80

That's All Folks!

JONATHAN KING

Volume Three of
his autobiography

First published in Great Britain in 2025.
Revvolution Publishing Limited.
Queensborough Studios, London W2 3SQ
United Kingdom
www.KingOfHits.com

Copyright © K G King 2025

The moral rights of K G King to be identified as
the author of the work has been asserted in accordance with
the Copyright, Designs and Patents Act of 1988.
All rights reserved.

Almost no characters in this book are fictitious.
But if you're alive please don't sue me.

All photos were taken by or are owned by K G King -
some origin public domain.

A CIP catalogue record for this book
is available from the British Library.

ISBN 978-1-8382072-9-8

Printed in Great Britain by JF Graphics

Typeset in Stempel Garamond

80

That's All Folks!

DEDICATIONS PAGE

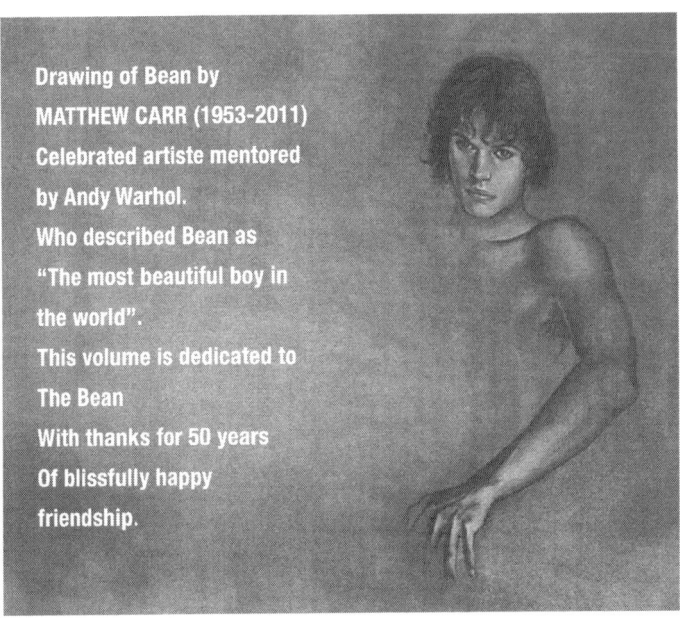

Drawing of Bean by
MATTHEW CARR (1953-2011)
Celebrated artiste mentored
by Andy Warhol.
Who described Bean as
"The most beautiful boy in
the world".
This volume is dedicated to
The Bean
With thanks for 50 years
Of blissfully happy
friendship.

Also to Janet Atkinson and my brothers.

Andy (in my arms) edited this volume.

Other books by Kenneth or Jonathan King include…

Bible Two;
The Booker Prize Winner;
65 My Life So Far;
70 FFFY;
Beware the Monkey Man (as Rex Kenny);
Death Flies, Missing Girls and Brigitte Bardot;
Three Months;
The Spirit Phone (as Kate Genifer);
Don't Go In;
Thomas Love Peacock Luv Tom; Guilty;
Not A Knee On The Neck;
Animal Farm - The Next Chapter;
The Polish Boy And The Pope.

They are all brilliant.

CONTENTS

Chapter One
Sex Before Sex - *3*

Chapter Two
History Can Change - Jimmy Savile and George Michael - *15*

Chapter Three
Eurovision and more Brits - *29*

Chapter Four
David Bowie - *41*

Chapter Five
Criminal Convictions; False Accusers; Case Study One - *55*

Chapter Six
Margaret Thatcher; The Brits; Top of the Pops and yet more Eurovision - *71*

Chapter Seven
More Case Histories from 2001 *85*

Chapter Eight
Sex with John Lennon; The Beatles and Brian Epstein *103*

Chapter Nine
Money - *115*

Chapter Ten
Rogue DJs - Kenny Everett and Chris Denning - *125*

Chapter Eleven
The Second Police Bite at my Cherry - *165*

Chapter Twelve
Helmi, Rupert Murdoch, Piers Morgan, Prince Andrew - *183*

Chapter Thirteen
Books, Films, Music and even Elton John - *197*

Chapter Fourteen
The Crime Of The Century - *209*

Chapter Fifteen
Senility, Alzheimers, Prison Life and Mr King - *223*

Chapter Sixteen
Johnny Reggae, Rod Stewart and the Skinheads - *233*

Chapter Seventeen
The CCRC, Police and Crime Commissioners and Victims - *247*

Chapter Eighteen
For Those About To Die - We Salute You - *259*

Chapter Nineteen
Private Investigators, Police and Crooked Lawyers - *279*

Chapter Twenty
I Am About To Die - *291*

JONATHAN KING

PREFACE

"You know, Barabbas", said John Lennon, looking down on me from his cross, "you really shouldn't be up here".

"I know", I replied, "I thought I'd gotten away with it".

"Well, we'd better move on, I suppose".

"What's next, then, John?".

"Death".

It's odd how dreams can be. And so often they are rooted in truth.

Let me start with an apology. It's a lie. I hope. Although **65 My Life So Far** was correct - and it continued to **70 FFFY - Five Further Fucking Years**. Now 80 - That's All Folks! takes me to the end of my exciting life, but it doesn't, I hope.

Yes, while none of us can anticipate when the Grim Reaper arrives at our door, black cowl, huge sharp scythe, silent but deadly as she always has been, I sincerely hope

80
That's All Folks!

to live for at least ten more years, until I'm 90, and would quite like to reach 100.

As long as my marbles remain intact and rolling and my poor old body refuses to succumb to aches and pains. Mind you, as I tell my younger friends, it's all a great adventure, isn't it? What comes next?

So there may even be a further Volume or two of my dodgy autobiography. Who knows? But for now - read on, with some brand new stories about celebrities or others who have passed away, or extensions of tales told, that I felt needed amplifying and expanding.

JONATHAN KING

Chapter 1

SEX BEFORE SEX

I assume it was natural, in the late forties, to play at SOLDIERS when one was a little boy.

I was a very little boy, having been born in December 1944, after three days of labour during which I poked my head out, surveyed the world outside and concluded it would be far safer to remain inside. The war didn't stop for a few months. A bomb threw me out of my cot.

After three days of agony, according to my mother, the doctors had decided to seize my head with forceps and I was delivered into London, England with only one nerve on my upper lip slightly damaged, giving me a rather attractive crooked smile. Years later Elvis Presley and others tried to perfect my sneer but none succeeded.

Tony, a neighbour boy of similar age, five or six, insisted we go into the woods to play SOLDIERS.

We lived, at the time, in Brookhurst Grange, a large mansion, now converted into three huge homes but then

80
That's All Folks!

entirely occupied by the King family. My father, George Farquhar Jones King, had served in the war. An American who had lived in England since a very young age, had been to school in England (Oundle) and joined up with the American Field Service when war broke out.

He was a Captain, promoted to Major and then to Lieutenant Colonel and had a very distinguished war, being captured by the Germans, escaped from a prisoner of war camp, served in the Middle East, was one of the first into Belsen when it was liberated and was much admired by those under him, as I found out after my mother died, when we got dozens of messages from soldiers who had served with him. He was awarded both the Croix de Guerre and the OBE, which I still have in my house.

After the war he became Managing Director of Tootals - the shirt and tie manufacturer - a company founded by my great uncle - by marriage only; his wife Giulia, had married Kenneth Lee, after whom I was named, and she was the sister of my father's mother in America. Another of my close relatives, my brother's Godfather, was Head of an advertising agency in America and had come up with the slogan, not for Tootals but for another shirt company, of LOOKS EVEN BETTER ON A MAN - worn, in pictures, by a cute, slim blonde girl, far too big for her and very sexy. Genius. The shirt sold millions as a result and Jock Elliott was rewarded and promoted.

The Lees lived in Lukyns, an even bigger mansion, next to Brookhurst. We visited them many times - they had one of the first televisions. I remember how excited we all were by the massive black and white screen.
Here comes Muffin; Muffin the Mule.

I go into much greater detail regarding my happy childhood in Volume One of my autobiography - 65 My Life So Far. Some here is bound to be repeated but most consists of events or details either avoided, glossed over or missing entirely, often because some of those involved were then alive and are now dead or even might have living family members, who might be offended. Some names that I felt I could not give, I can now, at least partially, reveal. And a lot has happened over the past 15 years that I can now detail at the ripe old age of 80.

So Tony and I went into the woods. Huge trees, grass, insects, birds that chirped and small animals - even some big animals. The odd deer scuttled past, and we once saw a fox who we called Rommel.

The English countryside is magnificent, particularly when the sun shines, partly because it usually rains, which encourages the growth and greenery of many species. In later life I've come to adore trees, which I suspect may be the most numerous species on earth if you include shrubs, bushes and so on. Friends say NO, there are more fish.

80
That's All Folks!

Or germs. But talking about germs, Germans were the enemy - the war having ended a mere few years earlier.

"Now", said Tony, "we must take down our shorts. Soldiers were often in the woods - actually forests in Germany. And they had to relieve themselves". To this day I'm not convinced soldiers wore shorts but Tony was older, more experienced and, I assumed, more knowledgeable about these things.

An obedient child, I pulled down my shorts, as he did. He then explained that, after vital functions had been completed, soldiers had to use their initiative, as far as cleaning themselves up afterwards was concerned.

A brief detour here. Toilet paper, in the first half of the last century, was very unpleasant stuff. Shiny, like grease proof paper, on one side and only slightly less rough on the other. Loose sheets in a box, not soft rolls like today.

I remember Mr Dean, at another school much later, had rationed paper, a habit from after the war, I suppose. We children had to go to him before visiting the WC, and we were only allowed three small sheets "One for cleaning, one for wiping and one for polishing" he used to say.

I remember once using the wrong side and learning that was for SMEARING. Not nice.

Anyway, Tony explained that "using your initiative" involved finding big, dead leaves and using them as toilet paper. He asked me to wipe his backside with a large leaf. He then offered to do the same for me, a kind suggestion which I chose to decline. We pulled up our shorts and returned home.

Another time, on another day, we went through the same routine but this time Tony asked me to push a dead leaf further inside and to follow it with another. Which I did. Several times. Again, he offered to do it for me, but once more I declined his kind proposal.

Later that day I was lying on my bed reading a comic, the Beano or the Dandy it would likely have been, when my mother came in, sat beside me and said "I've just had a telephone call from Tony's mother who was bathing him and found some dead leaves up his bottom. He said you put them there. Did you?".

"Yes".

"Why?"

"Because he asked me to".

I never saw Tony again. Looking back, I'm sure Tony confirmed my story; why wouldn't he? I hope in later life he found someone willing to push more than dead leaves up his bottom, if that was what they and he wanted. I do remember his full name but no need... no need. He may still be alive aged 80. And might prefer NOT to be identified as The Dead Leaf Boy.

The point being that, in the 1940s, this was considered

80
That's All Folks!

perfectly normal behaviour. Curiosity. Not sex. Nothing to do with sex.

I tell another story in 65 My Life So Far of the Headmaster's daughter at Bramshott Chase, with whom I experimented "because she liked it". Aged about 6 or 7. She was intrigued by the piece of loose, spare skin I had and I was intrigued by the extra orifice she had in its place..

Again - curiosity, not sex. And Michael, the cook's son who allowed me to examine him as a reward for "getting through" 20 cigarettes - but I didn't properly explain why I was fascinated by Michael's enormous penis - at least the size of my little finger compared to my tiny toothpick.

No; it wasn't a toothpick. It was more like a match stick and the reason I was intrigued was because mine did not have a foreskin and his did.

This was interesting. Why? Circumcision went on to rear its head later in my life. Indeed, at school we often used to try to guess which boys were Roundheads and which were Cavaliers. Even then it was a game, not remotely connected to sex. But at four or five I had not been informed of the basics of religion. In fact it seemed often to be a regional thing. Roundheads came from the South. Cavaliers were from the North. Later on it dawned on me that I was circumcised because most Americans were, and the paternal side of my family was, of course,

American.

Innocence throughout. Something that appears to have been lost in this Century, when such activities as those above could result in police investigation. I regret the loss of innocence and the sensible adults who dealt with curiosity exactly as they should have done, then, and still should do, now. The media and society wouldn't allow it, of course, in the 21st Century. Lock 'em up and throw away the key. That five year old is a potential pervert. Get 'em young, like the church. I bet these days small kids shout PAEDO at other kids instead of the old favourite QUEER.

I've told before of my first encounter with a Vile Pervert.

I arrived home one day from the local village school and announced to my mother that it had been a fantastic day because I'd been interviewed by the police.

"What about?".

"Mr Jones the handyman. They wanted to know if he'd ever come into the toilet when I was there".

"Why would he have wanted to do that?"

"Don't be silly, Mummy. He could have put his hands in my pockets when my shorts were down and stolen my pencils".

Innocence. Curiosity. Are children still like that? Or has the internet, with instant knowledge of the most

80
That's All Folks!

graphic kind, removed the slow progress towards the dawning of life? In the first few years of life I knew all about thieves and robbery.

I probably knew something about murder and killing - despite the fact that my parents' generation had been doing it on a massive scale all over Europe, Africa and as far away as Asia and Japan, it was taught to me that generally killing someone, or stealing from them, was a bad thing.

Not to be encouraged.

But those first few years of physical and emotional experimentation are vital and the online, brutal exposure these days simplifies everything, removes the tentative, subtle development. And I was very lucky that my parents and Tony's parents and the Masters at Bramshott Chase had the good sense to realise that children are curious and should not be punished for it.

Curiosity became sex for me in my first days at Stoke House in Seaford. I've told before of how I hated the place - my first proper boarding school with the vile Arthur Spring Rice Pyper - the headmaster who used to beat me for any excuse, one hand plunged deep into his trouser pocket, grunting and wheezing. But I didn't name X at the time - the boy who taught me about sex.

Nigel was very handsome, always smiling, slightly older than me and showed me how, if he rubbed me in a certain way, I could get a delightful feeling after a few minutes, quite a lot of minutes, actually, if I would do the same to him.

That was a revelation. Nigel died a few years ago so I can now use his name, though not his full name. He became a respected Governor at the minor public school that he went to, after Stoke. He grew a large beard. He never married. My gratitude to him is because he showed me that there was nothing wrong, if both parties enjoyed themselves, with such behaviour. I had yet to discover the many pitfalls that could come from sex, especially not the reinvention and exaggeration, often genuine and inspired by changes in society, especially by the media.

I was still pre-teen. But curiosity had turned into sex, which was to become one of the great joys of my life and linked with music, literature, friendship and love to be the corner stones of my 80 very happy, fulfilled years of existence.

In my experience the vast majority of teenage boys want some kind of sexual contact but the majority of teenage girls don't. Several of the girls I got to know in later life had suffered some kind of sexual abuse, from suggestions, often rejected, to activity, sometimes accepted for reasons other than desire, frequently wanting to please the abuser. Many times, sex with a female partner was stopped - by me - when I became aware they

80
That's All Folks!

were having problems emotionally. It never happened with males.

It's a very individual area, and needs both parties to behave honourably and honestly. Easier said than done.

Let's play a little game. It's called lateral thinking. I'll ask the questions and provide the answers.

Is there anything wrong with sex? No.

Don't qualify it or add stupid extras like "under certain circumstances". That can come later, if ever. Essentially no, there is nothing wrong with sex.

We all have our own desires and tastes. It is vital, for me, that the partner enjoys themselves. One reason why I've never paid for sex or been with a prostitute.

Having said that, there are times when a prostitute may be justifying their behaviour where, in reality, it is a way to satisfy their own desires. Which is one point. It is an individual thing. And by putting regulations on it generally, society is making Mistake Number One. Some people may get pleasure with a prostitute and, if so, why not?

And yet, like religion, like most things, we do need boundaries - particularly for the majority who are often incapable of making their own morality decisions.

It is wrong to kill or hurt or be violent towards another human being but there are circumstances. If you had met Hitler, for example. Or Stalin. Or a murderer about to slaughter your wife. Or Mariah Carey (for crimes against singing).

If sex is essentially rape, for instance, which need not always include physical violence but can be seduction with dishonesty, it is, for me anyway, morally wrong and no longer sex. It has moved into a category called VIOLENCE, and out of that described as sex.

But again that is only my personal opinion. Another aspect, of when it can be wrong, is when it breaks the law in any specific territory and for that I have to plead guilty. GUILTY. GUILTY. GUILTY.

Because then you are breaking the law of that chosen society and so, often, is your partner.

Until 1967 it was totally illegal to have sex with another male in the UK, no matter how old you were. Yet sex with a member of the opposite sex was legal (and encouraged) if both parties were over 16.

Absurd. When I became aware of this (watching the film VICTIM aged 15) I decided to ignore it. It was ridiculous. As a bisexual male, to whom gender was far less important than other qualities, it was bonkers. As long as my partner enjoyed it and wanted it, sex was fine.

I failed to realise that experts in the art of false allegations would, decades later, know that tweaking and adapting, let alone inventing, could still end up sending someone to prison. But I also failed to understand, back

80
That's All Folks!

then, that sometimes persuading someone to do something they wanted to do and enjoyed as a teenager, might become different in memory and might affect future relationships, especially if society, as it did, changed position on the act years later. When media tells you something (inevitably "a good story") you often believe it and adapt your recollections accordingly.

I do wonder - are there no longer any teenagers who would like some kind of sexual experience, if consensual, with somebody else? Should that automatically be illegal? If so, why? Yes children must be taught how to reject such advances if they don't want to proceed and how to differ polite requests from brutal ones. Yes - everyone needs to learn. But it's not simple; everybody is different. Making laws and rules based on extreme positions only provokes exaggeration and inflation in today's media world.

Anyway, enough of all that. Experimentation in 2025 is often a crime, so you or they SHOULD NOT DO IT!

JONATHAN KING

Chapter 2

HISTORY CAN CHANGE; JIMMY SAVILE & GEORGE MICHAEL

I've written about my sole social encounter with Jimmy Savile in Volume Two of this autobiography - 70 FFFY. It tells you that I consider the man to have been virtually a saint. But this is a good place to discuss the making of monsters. Not just by the media - which will do anything to create or inflate a great story - but we, the people. We love monsters. Or rather, we love to hate monsters. We have neither the time nor the inclination for depth of thought in 2025, particularly on people or topics that have nothing to do with us.

Oh, Hitler and Stalin tangentially affected lives in Great Britain and America, though far more if you were German or Russian. Attila the Hun was probably lovely to his wives and families and may even have been nice to animals but unless you were one of the races he butchered, who cares?

80
That's All Folks!

We have far more important subjects to consider. What's for dinner? Are we doing our jobs right? Should we get married? Are our children learning? Can we conceal our porn habit from our mother? Which car should we buy or which house should we rent? Should we tell our boss she has BO?

So we all love the odd monster to hate in our spare time - and you couldn't get much odder than Jimmy Savile. When he was one of the most popular figures in Britain, inexplicably, he was very odd with that ghastly thinning, yellow dyed hair, those absurd track suits, the catchy but irritating phrases, the constant cigar. The Rolls Royce.

Yes, you've spotted it. I had and have something in common with Savile, as I am seen in one of my many Rolls Royces. And I, too, had limited talent - at least as a singer - but the ability to make the most of it by adopting gimmicks and promoting myself and my projects. So I do know about creating stars. I was a star once, promoting products, manipulating the media.

And I know about being monstered.

Was Savile a monster? I don't think so, but read 70 FFFY.

However they also like to create idols. And now that he's gone I might as well tell you about my personal impressions of George Michael, who became an idol partly because of me but who, very much, had feet of clay.

In the 1980s I was a "consultant" to a couple of record companies. A consultant is someone who is paid a great deal for doing very little.

It started in the 1970s. 10cc had, after three years with my UK Records, decided that they wanted to move away from my label, where I was paying them a tiny royalty, having explained that it would cost me a fortune to make them globally as big as they deserved to be. I would only be breaking even by Year Three, would make a big profit in Year Four and an absolute fortune in Year Five. This made sense to us all - they were an unknown, nameless band without a hit. I was a label, which needed success and could afford to invest in them. They not only agreed but were delighted.

So when they got big, as happens with most artistes, they decided they wanted to move, for far more money. The new label, Phonogram, paid me a large sum, with an over ride on all future tracks. One song, technically recorded whilst they were still contracted to me, was I'm Not In Love which earns me quite hefty royalties to this day.

At this point, totally disillusioned by the morality of artistes and their managers and, naturally, lawyers, I decided to run down my label and leave the music business. After all, if you have an agreed, contracted deal

80
That's All Folks!

for five years and after three years of expense people decide to cancel the arrangement, what is the point? I really didn't enjoy the administrative part anyway, even the creative producer element where I pointed out and suggested musical, lyrical and sound changes to the finished product - which I did a lot for 10cc. I was essentially the fifth member.

No; fuck it. I hated being A LABEL BOSS. Drop it.

One of my friends was a man called Dick Asher, who ran CBS (later Sony) in the UK. He was a huge supporter of mine and also, I remember, of Mike Batt who had the Wombles hits, Katie Melua and many others - my favourite of his songs was Bright Eyes by Art Garfunkel.

Dick persuaded me to accept a highly paid consultancy to advise him at CBS. I remember in the 1980s, by which time Dick was running America, telling him not to drop Michael Jackson, a very expensive artiste who all his executives hated - Jackson then produced the Thriller album which vindicated my advice. His executives wanted the vast advances given to him to be devoted to their own dreadful artistes.

Which reminds me of another story - at this time my US lawyer was a lovely man called Paul Marshall who had become a dear, close, personal friend; it was he who had warned me, when I arrived in America, to avoid three New Yorkers at the time - Roy Cohn, Donald Trump and

Benjamin Netanyahu. "Bad people" he said.

Paul represented a new artiste and asked me to get her an audition with CBS - I did so though, again A&R people were very negative about doing anything for a "consultant", especially someone who "had the ear" of the boss. Head of A&R, Micky Eichner, a nice man, went to see her himself and sent me his considered opinion.

"Pretty girl; can't sing".

So I told Paul to take her to a friend of mine, Clive Davis at Arista, a label he'd just started, having left CBS. He did very nicely with WHITNEY HOUSTON.

Some years later she was rehearsing How Will I Know on The Brits which I was presenting. After she finished the song it came to me and I said (in the empty rehearsal - NOT in the show) "I think I've just fallen in love". She turned and gave me the most fabulous smile. She was a sweet girl and I seriously regret obeying my "Never mix business and pleasure" motto as far as she was concerned.

Anyway back to another star.

One of my jobs was co-ordinating between the UK and the US companies.

A little group called WHAM was getting success in Great Britain but had not really exploded in the USA, although they had done quite well, but the British label Epic - a division of CBS - really believed that George Michael, half of WHAM, was potentially a global

80
That's All Folks!

superstar. I met with Al Teller, then running the Columbia label in the USA under Dick Asher, to ask him, please, to work George's records in the States.

"He's not very American", he said, "but I tell you what. If you can persuade the UK to break this VERY US-only track I've just picked up, I'll make this George Michael kid, for you over here, a top priority". Records and artistes only ever broke in America if the record company devoted an enormous amount of money and time to promotion, marketing and (often buying) radio plays.

He then played me "You've Gotta Fight For Your Right To Party" by the Beastie Boys. That band meant little in the UK though they were big in the States. I was delighted. It was a dead cert smash in any country and would be a hit wherever released.

"Deal" I said. And the rest is history.

I'd met George Michael a couple of times at the CBS offices in Soho Square and once or twice in trendy restaurants. A very quiet, shy boy. Obviously gay but firmly in the closet. Signed to a production company called Innervision which, like nearly all artistes, he dumped the moment WHAM started to become successful. His manager for a time was Simon Napier Bell, a friend of mine who had managed a group called John's Children a decade earlier, which included a boy called

Marc Bolan who I championed in print when he made a record called Deborah as T Rex.

Simon, later in life, wrote some terrific books about the music world in the last century. Thoroughly recommended. He also wrote, with my friend Vicky Wickham, the lyrics for an Italian song called You Don't Have To Say You Love Me, which became a huge hit for Dusty Springfield.

As George grew more and more popular he began to believe his own image. He was a global superstar. When I took over as Producer of The Brits, the British equivalent of the Grammys, named by me as an acronym for the British Recording Industry Trusts Show - George was booked as the star of the show in 1991.

He would perform one of his hits - I think Freedom 90 - as the finale.

He was delighted by this. We organised the special set, dramatic explosions and effects.

A couple of days before the live show was due to be broadcast by the BBC I got a call from his Manager, at the time Andy Stephens I think, a friend who had been the Epic label manager at CBS, saying sadly, George was sick and would not be able to attend.

Horrified, I managed to book instead a young band EMF, who had a massive hit at the time, Unbelievable. As it happens, they were terrific. I changed the running order

80
That's All Folks!

of the programme and it worked magnificently - the show was a huge success.

The Brits had collapsed in 1989, during a farcical show in which the hosts, Mick Fleetwood and Samantha Fox, had been chosen because of the difference in height between tall Mick and tiny Sam. An odd reason for choice of presenters but typical of many businesses where those at the top have no clue about what actually matters in the chosen industry.

I myself had hosted the 1987 Brits when I named them - before that they were called the Daily Mirror Rock And Pop Awards Show, if I remember correctly. The DMRAPAS was a less catchy acronym.

That show had been so successful that the BPI had decided to move it to a bigger venue (mistake) and to hire a far less expensive presenter - Noel Edmonds. The 1988 Brits over ran and was not a success so, for 1989, they took on different producers, who made the above decision on hosts.

Reflecting the growing trend, as in Positive Discrimination, to support hires for reasons other than abilities or talent. This trend has grown over the years, leading to massive support for people of different colour, religion, sexuality and disability over the less important (sarcasm) area of skill. I actually think Positive Discrimination, which later morphed into WOKE, is responsible for much of the mess society has gotten into this century.

Anyway after the disaster of 1989, when the poor hosts were unable to read the autocue or to string words together on camera, I was begged to return for the 1990 and subsequent shows. They offered me a fortune and a deal for life. Nobody else wanted to touch the poisoned chalice that The Brits had become. People today have forgotten what a titanic catastrophe the Sam and Mick show had been. I took over and the 1990 show was a great success.

The day before the 1991 show I was informed that George Michael was well enough to attend - just to accept his Award for Album of the Year.

Of course, the reality was that he couldn't be bothered to turn up to sing but was happy enough to pop along for a few minutes to accept the prestigious prize. Allowing him time to go cottaging, I presumed.

He arrived and was brought to the side of the stage, where I was waiting with my brother Andy. I mention this because it was also Andy who accompanied me to the Stoke Mandeville hospital day with Jimmy Savile.

Andy's jaw dropped when he saw my polite (sarcasm) confrontation with George, who was clearly perfectly well and had been for weeks.

I told him he was a disgrace to the music world. He

80
That's All Folks!

was a diva and a silly queen who was so proud to win this award - did he know how many awards I had won over the decades, before his tiny little testicles had descended, if that had, by now, actually occurred? Was he aware of the amount of people whose lives had been disrupted? Set designers, sound people, publicity, cameras…? Cancelling a performance that had been contracted weeks before, just because he wasn't in the mood?

As it happened we'd got the No1 hit of the moment, Unbelievable, with EMF, a young group of enthusiastic kids who rehearsed, turned up on time and got a standing ovation as opposed to a jaded old fairy making dull but expensive videos with no imagination, who was high on drugs most of the time.

By the time he went on stage to collect his award from my friend Robin Gibb of the BeeGees, who had also witnessed this confrontation and was highly amused by it, he was white and shaking, like a small boy chastised by a strict Headmaster.

After the show which was, again, a huge success - featuring some unsigned acts like CARTER USM, to the fury of the major labels - I wrote to George's manager and label boss, chastising them for letting minor artistes with limited talent treat people like this and urging them to give him a dressing down, if not punishing him.

I also wrote an even more stiff reprimand to George

Michael, who complained vehemently to all the executives concerned. They backed me 100%. But none of them had any control over him. Stars are allowed 100% misbehaviour, even though they usually contribute less than 10% to success. They surround themselves with YES men and women who do not dare complain, or even suggest.

However, I must say I was horrified when he was set up by police in Los Angeles. We all knew he was a cottage queen - several friends had seen him cottaging in London. Cottaging was a tradition for gays and bisexuals stretching back centuries. Whenever public toilets were invented, men would arrive in them. seeking partners. I once, in the 1960s, saw a famous actor next to the Editor of a national tabloid newspaper pleasuring each other in a toilet (cottage) off Leicester Square.

It bears repeating that until 1967 any male to male sexual contact was forbidden by law, punished by prison sentences and disgrace and often causing blackmail or, worse, suicide. I urge anyone unaware of this to watch the brilliant Dirk Bogarde film VICTIM. Dirk was himself gay but firmly in the closet, as one had to be, and it was terrifically brave of him to play this part - which he did, incidentally, magnificently.

Because of the situation with society, many cottagers were bisexual males, often married with families, who

80
That's All Folks!

knew of nowhere else where they could enjoy that part of their sexuality. And why not? No harm in it. Consenting adults in the "privacy" of a public toilet.

I was in my New York home in 1998 when I saw on the news that George had been arrested in Los Angeles for cottaging. With a rather dishy young cop - this behaviour was known as entrapment and was, in many jurisdictions, illegal.

I had a meeting early that morning with Donny Ienner, then running Columbia Records. I was no longer a consultant to the company but still met all top executives regularly. Donny often played me tracks long before release, to get my opinion. Many executives did this. They had become friends and wanted my thoughts. I remember Donny playing me a very early demo by Destiny's Child and - before letting anybody else hear it - wanted me to hear Livin' La Vida Loca by Ricky Martin, saying "A Front Pager?".

At the time I ran The Tipsheet and a Front Page selection of a future release often guaranteed global success. "Oh yes" I replied - "thanks for playing it to me".

George was suing CBS for not working his records hard enough in America and Donny was, unfairly, the prime target for his anger.

I broke the news of his arrest to Donny and was most

impressed by his reaction. He was horrified. How dare they do this kind of entrapment? Police should be ashamed of themselves.

Donny was a very heterosexual male, married with children, deeply conservative yet liberal and tolerant in all the areas of life that mattered. Not for one second did he display any pleasure at the downfall of his enemy. He was dismayed that this sort of thing could happen. And totally sympathetic to George. He was, incidentally, a very fine music man, mentored originally by my dear friend, mentioned above, Clive Davis.

I thought George handled his entrapment brilliantly. Full of admiration for his response.

But it didn't affect my opinion of him. He was a silly queen who should have known better how to behave, when fame arrived.

80
That's All Folks!

JONATHAN KING

Chapter 3

EUROVISION AND MORE BRITS.

From one camp experience to another - yes, gays have been a massive part of the music world, as well as life in general. My friend Michael Summerton was delighted that my mother knew the singer and writer of a hit from the 30s or 40s or so - I think he was called Dougie Byng and the lyric went "I'm a tree, I'm a tree, Everybody wants to come up me". Gays in music. There's a book to be written about that.

There would have been no Beatles without gay Brian Epstein. Larry Parnes. Joe Meek. Andrew Loog Oldham (though his "gay" image was fake).

I constantly feel the need to apologise, here in Volume Three of my autobiography, to those who have read the first or second volumes - 65 My Life So Far or 70 FFFY. You may know some of the stories in here.

One of the joys of my life has been the variety of aspects of it, and one of the things I achieved was running

80
That's All Folks!

and winning the British entry for the Eurovision Song Contest. I go into detail in the first volume but I wanted to describe the joy of this bizarre annual event. You'll spot new anecdotes throughout 80. Not just about Eurovision.

And so much has happened since 2014 that require updates in 2025.

The Eurovision Song Contest was one of the very first global media events. Just as television was starting, and only then involving seven European countries and broadcasters in 1956, it was then won by Switzerland who, oddly, won last year as I write, and are hosting this year in 2025, in Basel.

I predict AUSTRIA will win. This is cheating - by the time this tome was edited and published the rather ordinary Austrian song had won.

I was never much of a fan of Eurovision. The songs were generally awful and the acts very middle-of-the-road. But the concept, culminating in votes announced slowly in order, made for exciting viewing. And as the years went by I found myself liking the odd entry - the Allisons in 1961, the UK entry with Are You Sure? was a real hit. Gigliola Cinquetti, for Italy in 1964 won with Non Ho L'Eta and started my interest in foreign language hits, which gave me masses of later hits like Una Paloma Blanca and Gloria.

So when David Liddiment, then Head of

JONATHAN KING

Entertainment at the BBC, begged me to take over finding a British entry in 1995, as opposed to taking over Top of the Pops, which I had really wanted to do, I grudgingly accepted. And I ended up finding the last UK winner to date in Love Shine A Light by Katrina and the Waves in 1997, for which result I was made the UK **Man of the Year** by the British music industry. Although I felt that our previous entry, Ooh Aah Just A Little Bit by Gina G was a far better entry. It only came eighth but I still consider it the perfect Eurovision track.

I made many friends through my Eurovision involvement. I've attended several events since and it is very strange but terribly important.

All the media news crews cover it and love it because it is SOO trivial and unimportant. It's got sillier and sillier. Instead of reporting on wars and killing and deaths and famines, these hard bitten hacks get their noses into a bouquet of roses. They laugh and giggle and let their hair down.

There are literally millions of fans, some of whom know every detail of every entry, every artiste and every result. Many have become friends but they are not anoraks or train spotters and many have top jobs. One was right at the peak of Heathrow immigration - now retired, still a friend. I remember Tony Benn, a fine left wing politician, being on my Talk Radio show and during

80
That's All Folks!

a commercial break said to me - "I must tell you that you're doing a brilliant job running Eurovision". "Are you a fan?" I asked. "Oh yes - isn't everyone?". Ken Livingstone ditto.

A lot are queens. It does seem to attract the gay community as Eurovision is essentially a camp event - as every important gathering should be. How much more fun would a G7 conference be if all the men wore makeup and drag? Mind you, Starmer or Trump or Putin in lipstick is a Horror Show idea.

I'm quite a celebrity if I go to the week of the shows, wherever they may be, as many of the hardened fans (ooh Matron) know that, if it hadn't been for me, the UK might have pulled out in the 1990s.

Alan Yentob, then the BBC1 boss, hated it, just as my friend Michael Grade, years earlier, had hated and cancelled both Miss World and Dr Who. Yentob - or Botney, as Private Eye cleverly called him - was on the verge of dropping it when I took over. He thought it was too low brow; not artistic; appealing to viewers he didn't want.

He once cornered me at the BBC and said "Jonathan I cannot tell you how much I hate you for reviving Eurovision. I was determined to cancel the damn thing and now the ratings have gone through the roof, I can't".

"Glad to have been of assistance Botney", I replied.

JONATHAN KING

Alan died recently. I liked him and he did make a lot of great shows. Mind you, he admired Janet Street Porter; a serious flaw in judgement.

Due to finding real hits as the UK entries, and eventually winning, my era had seen viewer ratings explode, destroying all hope of killing it off.

Each year's event takes place in whichever country won the previous year. It's rumoured to be very expensive to put on and the media assumes, as a result, countries don't want to host it. This is rubbish. It makes a fortune - not just the TV show but for hotels, restaurants, taxis, airports - and of course merchandising, T shirts etc.

When we won in 1997 I offered to buy the rights to host it the next year. NO WAY howled the BBC - "it makes us and Birmingham", where they hosted it, on my suggestion, "a fortune". Actually that year I had been told that, due to my winning it at last, I could choose the host city. I chose Belfast - thinking it would really help that wonderful city and those fantastic people but the "troubles" still existed and security concerns understandably blocked it, so Birmingham, a very under rated place, was my second choice.

For several weeks - rehearsals, filming, sets and so on - the chosen city is packed. Media adores it. Interviews galore. Sadly, not many artistes emerge from it, though Abba did, of course. Oddly, a group we had picked up

80
That's All Folks!

the publishing for, before they won for Sweden in 1974 with Waterloo.

There are dinners and meetings and much hilarity. Although the UK hasn't won since my era we did host it in 2023 in Liverpool and actually Sam Ryder should have won that previous year. Ukraine did with a political sympathy vote, as it had just been invaded. Sam's strong song in 2022 came second in Turin and, as Ukraine was otherwise occupied by Putin's forces at the time, the UK was asked to put the show on in 2023.

I went to the Turin event and had a great time. Eurovision never fails to impress. Huge TV events take an enormous amount of planning and resources and reflect the very best in all aspects of entertainment. Right across the board the logistics are incredible and I find them impressive.

Credit is not often given to those behind the scenes. The actual acts are less important - rather like the music and other entertainment, where it's often the producers, arrangers, engineers, song writers, managers and others who are truly responsible for hits, the actors in films and plays have very little to contribute, and it's the same with television.

We credit the stars but where would they be without lighting, microphones, makeup, hairstylists…???

That may be one reason why I so admire Eurovision.

But I'm also sad that it has become less and less of a song contest. It now depends almost entirely on the visual performance. I always thought a real hit would cut through. Wrong - or Just A Little Bit would have won. It ended up going to No1 and even selling millions in America, a country often untouched by Eurovision.

But Katrina, bless her, knew how to sell a less good song visually. Which was why Love Shine A Light got more 12 points, in ratio to countries taking part, that ever before or since. Every year Katrina is asked about the contest and every year, without fail, credits me for it, which cannot be an easy thing to do. One of my main interests in Eurovision, as with going to American political conventions. It is spotting the tiny dramas that go on behind the scenes and admiring the massive technical and artistic achievements.

Several aspects of the show each year highlight the changes in the larger music industry.

These days, as executives are less and less able to find mass appeal talent or hits, the industry has specialised in concentrating on acts that appeal to specific fan bases. So whilst artistes like Taylor Swift and BTS can sell millions to their fans who go to concerts, buy merchandise and stream tracks again and again, very few touch the lives or the ears of the majority of people. Indeed most ordinary people could not even name the title of a BTS song, let

80
That's All Folks!

alone hum it.

Those running the contests in each country are equally unable to find mass appeal entries. So, as a result, the winner often owes more to staging, performance and gimmicks like hair styles or costumes than to the music. It was always thus (remember Bucks Fizz and the skirts?) but is now almost totally visual rather than musical.

Society has also changed. These days most listeners like something instant, catchy and immediate. Again, the element of Boom Bang A Bang was always a part of Eurovision but it now dominates more than ever. Superficiality in society is mirrored in taste in music.

The Brits just revealed they were moving the annual event to Manchester due to the falling ratings - just over 2 million for 2025 whereas, when I produced them, they topped 10 million. NOOO - mistake - once again made by people who simply do not understand the reality of the industry. They will never get big names to present the awards (a minor duty) if they have to stay overnight in Manchester. They seem unaware that the reason for the ratings slump is that there is no mass appeal music these days - resulting in little viewer interest. They think that the huge popularity of bands like Oasis means millions will tune in - not understanding that Oasis only have a few fans. Though they will pack out stadiums and stream billions, they have no appeal to the majority. The image - like so many - is totally media created and fake. The billions are just millions, globally; a minuscule minority.

I would like the Eurovision Song Contest to revert to the quality of the song. The melody and the lyric should gain extra points for imagination or inspiration. Yes, so should the performance and the originality. And I'd like to see artistes emerging - only Abba and Celine Dion really came from the contest and Celine's win for Switzerland in 1988 had little to do with her eventual success.

Real music stars like Bruce Springsteen and Michael Jackson are never "found" through Eurovision. Why not? With that massive global audience, these days including places like Australia (Eurovision???), it could be a window for genuine talent.

And there is that other appalling encroachment - politics taking over. Example - Ukraine winning with a very average song - actually Sam Ryder's UK entry, which came second in 2022, should have won.

Banning Russia. Why? What has the Russian invasion of another country to do with music? Israel NOT being banned when they invaded Gaza - correct, as it had nothing to do with music, but if Russia got banned, why not Israel?

It was like Djokovic being banned from playing tennis

80
That's All Folks!

in Australia because he decided NOT to be vaccinated against Covid. A personal health decision in no way connected to sport. Absurd.

The cross contamination of areas of entertainment, sports and other areas is stupid and damages the quality and potential of the contenders. It's like positive discrimination, which, as I've mentioned, I hate. Hiring someone for reasons other than their ability to perform the function is ridiculous. Equally, someone's skin colour, gender, sexuality or religion should not affect such a decision.

Eurovision, like society, needs to adapt. Like Awards Shows - equally stuck in an old, dead format. Is there Climate Change? Of course there is. What causes it? Many things - and concentrating on one area in trying to stop it is a waste of time, expense and effort. Adapt to the possible changes. Don't build cities on flood plains or over earthquake faults. Colonise areas that will NOT be hit by tsunamis or hurricanes or tornados.

Yes, there will always be silly, pointless, hopeless Eurovision entries and indeed some will win. Yes, there are reasons to stop poisoning our oceans with plastic - unconnected to "climate change". Yes - the answer is to **adapt** without throwing out the baby with the bath water.

Why is humanity so unable to mix solutions?

JONATHAN KING

Everything requires sensible, artistic, creative adaption. And the Eurovision Song Contest, a marvellous way of bringing humans together, is a prime example of needing good, clever changes. So are The Brits. So is the music industry globally. And entertainment, universally. But what do I know?

80
That's All Folks!

Chapter 4

DAVID BOWIE

In 1965 I was approached by Bill Harry to write a weekly column on music for his and Virginia's publication Music Echo. This was actually, I thought, the best paper - better than the New Musical Express or Melody Maker or Disc, with whom Music Echo merged in 1966.

Bill was a Scouser, had been at the same school with my friend John Lennon and was partly funded, I think, by my friend Brian Epstein. I was still an undergraduate at Trinity College, Cambridge, refusing huge offers to go on tour as second on the bill to my idol, Gene Pitney, as I wanted to complete my education and get my degree which I eventually did - Master of Arts in English Literature.

But it was more my ability to spot talent, and willingness to condemn records I didn't like, that attracted Bill, I think; probably prompted by Brian. Anyway, whilst my first hit was still on the charts I

80
That's All Folks!

started the column in Music Echo - at the same time writing a weekly page in the Cambridge magazine Varsity called King's Parade, for Editor Paul Medlicott who became a friend and remains so to this day. Other friends at Varsity included Simon Hoggart who went on to be a top Guardian writer and a very good one too. My time as a writer has been, and continues to be, a very happy one, in tandem with music, TV and radio - all part of what I decided I was - a **COMMUNICATOR**.

It was quite unusual in the 1960s for a "pop star", which was what I then was, also to be a journalist, let alone a Cambridge undergraduate. My writing culminated in a weekly page in The Sun in the 1980s, as well as for many other national and international publications though some, not I, I must add, consider this, the third volume of my autobiography, to be the peak, the artistic pinnacle of my daubed endeavours. The Mount Everest of my scribbling sessions.

And, just as I failed to discuss many people and topics in Volumes One and Two, because many people were still alive or topics had not, by then, happened - so the subsequent deaths of celebrities has prompted numerous requests for greater detail on superstars. And possibly the most IN DEMAND of that is David Bowie.

Wendy Leigh was one of the many writers I got to know in the 1960s and she was aware of how close I had been to Bowie in his early days; she printed a small amount in her biography of him in 2014, after doing several interviews with me. Rather brave of her, I thought, as by then I had become Persona Non Grata in the world of publishing. Like everything else, valuable, first hand information is neglected if social and media mores have been offended.

In late 1965 I was sent, amongst the hundreds of other singles, in those days, early promotion copies of releases by all the labels. Already by then I was considered one of the most important critics - a kind of Michelin Guide spotter of up and coming talent - and I did manage to listen to all of them in between studying Byron, Dickens, Peacock and Shakespeare at my college Trinity, in which, when I left a couple of years later, I left a note with the porter to give to the Prince of Wales, coming up to replace me - "Your Highness; as a King steps down, a Prince comes up - welcome to Cambridge".

All those cherished vinyl copies are currently being sold off online to raise funds for my retirement and pay the wealth of medical and legal bills that seem to pile up, after you reach 80.

One single on the Pye label caught my ears. It was called Can't Help Thinking About Me by David Bowie and the Lower Third and I loved it.

So much so that I devoted my column to it, predicting

80
That's All Folks!

this was real talent.

The record did nothing. Nobody played it; nobody bought it.

But it prompted a call from the boy himself. One of his managers, Ken Pitt, was living just around the corner from my flat at the time in Dorset Street. Could he come round and thank me in person for the rave review? Sure.

Then started an interesting time. David, who declared himself gay, knew I was bisexual and wanted me to have sex with him.

I declined. Again and again. For a start I did not believe in mixing the areas of business and pleasure. Also I was nervous about having intimate exchanges with someone who was doing so with many others. It struck me as unsanitary, unwise and unhygienic. But, mainly, because I was not attracted to him physically at all. He had, at the time, terrible teeth. He had eyes of different colours - a total turn off for me. He clearly wasn't gay. His body was skinny and bony - I saw it naked many times. And the ultimate no-no. He only wanted to have sex with me because he felt it would further his career.

It wouldn't have. But we became friends. I gave him lots of advice - on his approach. On his song writing. About his business partners such as Ken Pitt, with whom he had, by then, moved in. But he never succeeded in seducing me and eventually gave up trying.

JONATHAN KING

Personally I found such a motivation highly unattractive. Even when, as I came across later in life, it is prompted by a genuine desire to please someone, it totally turns me off. One of the most physically attractive races on the planet is the Thai. Not only gorgeous. I've seen elderly beggars on the streets of Bangkok with the cheekbones of a top model. But they have lovely natures too. And most of them, both genders, want to please ME sexually whereas my pleasure, totally, is to please THEM.

Many times I've come across beautiful Thais of all three genders and never have found myself sexually interested. Many became and remain friends.

Strange though. Many times I have been rejected sexually, yet have gone on to be dear friends with those who turned me down. David Jones or Bowie was the one and only time that I turned the proposer down. And though we spent a great deal of time together in 1966, I would never have described David as a real friend.

Wendy Leigh never quite believed me, when I told her I turned him down. By then he was a superstar and considered highly attractive. Of course it would have been a much better story. Yet again, proof that every single word in this volume is true. I know several people who knew stars in their early days and most of them would never capitalise through inventing or exaggerating such stories. But there are millions out there who do, and

80
That's All Folks!

make fortunes from it.

A casual encounter with a member of the Royal Family, for example, and a hasty selfie to show Mom, can bring in millions in the future, if you espouse that kind of morality.

David got involved with a mime artiste called Lindsay Kemp. I've never seen the appeal of mime. All that "feeling imaginary walls" stuff. One night I was just dozing off in my flat in St Andrews Mansions when my phone went. It was David, in somewhere like Golders Green, in a show with Kemp.

"Nobody's here. Please come down".

No - I was just going to sleep. He went on and on, begging me. David could be very persuasive when he needed something. Finally I got dressed, drove all the way to Golders Green, watched the awful show, told him I hated it and gave him a lift back to Dorset Street.

In later life I often reminded him of this.

Some time later, it must have been in 1969 or 1970, I was having dinner with Alan Fluff Freeman, an old friend who had supported me since Day One and was one of the Big Four DJs in the 1960s - David Jacobs, Jimmy Savile and Pete Murray were the other three. Pete at time of writing (2025) is still with us.

At another table was David Bowie with his guitarist, who had long, blonde hair. David, if I remember rightly, was wearing a dress. So might have been Mick Ronson, the musician. He rushed up to the table and gave me a kiss and said "It's all just about to happen for me".

At the time I felt almost as though he had made a pact with the Devil. He was so totally certain and convinced, yet there was an emptiness about him. Whilst he was still sweet and affectionate I got the impression that I no longer mattered to him. That he had, somehow, linked up with a greater being. If you consider Satan a greater being. If your driving purpose in life is to succeed, I suppose he might be.

And so then, of course, he really DID happen. Part of the early 1970's GLAM ROCK world, seemingly bisexual, wearing makeup, getting even more influenced by the appalling Kemp; truly theatrical. Yet some terrific music too; some classic songs.

For me one of the bad sides of David became his willingness to emulate others. He was far too ready to adapt his style, rather like, decades later, Madonna.

If I covered a song, as I did often - example; my version of It's The Same Old Song by The Weathermen, totally unlike the fantastic Four Tops original, which had flopped in the UK, whereas mine was a big hit - I did it MY way. In that case using a solo violin playing the bass line.

David made a single called The Laughing Gnome,

80
That's All Folks!

which was pure Anthony Newley, a big artiste in the 60s - which didn't need to be like Newley but that was Bowie's trick. A chameleon. The single flopped until it was re-released a few years later by Decca, when he had happened, in 1973.

I think that was my overwhelming thought about David. Ambition. From that first day in 1966, he only wanted to succeed. He didn't mind how, where or when. It drove him in every way. Not an attractive quality in a human being. Seriously affecting any personal relationships.

He was also, as it happened, very talented. I recorded one of his songs, The Prettiest Star, with my protege Simon Turner who went on to become close to Angie Bowie, David's first wife.

Cut to 1985. I really didn't like David's version of Dancing In The Street that he'd done with Mick Jagger. In fact it was the video - two middle aged men dad dancing - that I hated. As it happens I didn't like the whole Band Aid/Live Aid thing, feeling that the music quality was low and forgiven by others - charity - and that the hype behind it would cause an increase in deaths, as donated funds would end up in the pockets of corrupt customs officials instead of reaching the starving, since most came from deflected money normally pledged to decent charities like Oxfam, The Red Cross, Save The

Children and my favourite, Medecins Sans Frontieres.

That was exactly what happened. Another Deal With The Devil went wrong - this time by Bob Geldof; look what happened to Paula Yates.

The only artiste to come out of Live Aid well, as they had rehearsed a Greatest Hits medley that sounded great and boosted sales astronomically, was Queen. My old friend Reg Dwight, Elton John, who decided to speak to me again a couple of years later, after I had dared to criticise the event, said "I decided life's too short". "It certainly is in Africa" I replied.

A few years passed. I was filming a series of Entertainment USA, the phenomenally successful BBC series, and David was doing a tour - the Glass Spider - and happened to be in concert near us in California. We set up a filming interview for before his show.

The crew and I drove out to Annaheim and were given a dressing room backstage to erect cameras and lights and the rest. David arrived with a posse of assistants clucking like hens, flapping their hands, bowing and scraping. That was always a bad sign. The bigger the star, the more they fell for their own image and tended to believe that they were superior and required dozens of helpers to get them through the day and take care of minor functions like obtaining drugs and getting the stars to interviews on time.

80
That's All Folks!

David sat in the chair provided. "Hello dear", I said, proffering a hand. In days gone by it would have been a hug and a kiss. He looked away. Another bad sign.

I sat down. Sadly before the cameras were running, he looked at me, said "you are a fat shit", got up and walked away, the minions scampering behind him in panic, chickens escaping the fox.

I giggled. Not good TV, since we'd not captured it all on film, but a great column for The Sun, about which Editor Kelvin MacKenzie later called me and said "best fucking column ever written".

I later found out, from my friend Peter Frampton, who was playing guitar on the tour, that it had been dogged by problems because of an amount of "white powder". The thin white duke took on a whole new meaning.

We didn't bother to stay for the show, which sounded like "not my kind of thing" at all. Pretentious and without the hits. He was working with Toni Basil whose one hit, Mickey, was amongst my most despised tracks of all time.

I loved Peter, who I called Hampton, after the cockney rhyming slang Hampton Wick, and knew from the 60s.

Peter was another of my sexual failures. Absolutely gorgeous in The Herd but not interested in me sexually at all and had a girlfriend (Mary?) with whom he was very happy and active. They often used to stay in my flat and once, I remember, I was in hospital, nursing an ulcer, and he insisted on bringing his parents, teachers, in to visit me, so I could persuade them that it was perfectly acceptable and normal, in that era, for boys to sleep with girls.

He was only 16 or 17 and both parents felt he was far too young to be indulging in that kind of liberal behaviour. Plus they were far from convinced by their young son spending so much time in the dodgy world of music.

I succeeded in persuading them all was fine and that Peter was destined for great success and he was very grateful. My educational position - I was still at Cambridge - held far greater sway than my pop status. Owen, Peter's Dad, used to teach 14 year old David Bowie or Jones, as he then was.

Another asset was that I didn't do drugs - still don't. Neither did Peter, especially not on the Glass Spider tour. I was never a normal pop person.

David died a decade ago. I never saw him again. Mutual friends tell me he sobered up and found love with Iman. As I've described, we were never that close personally though I suspect he thought we were closer than we were. But I helped him enormously in the early days. I suspect, like many others, without my early support he would never have become a star.

There are so many books about David Bowie but very few from those who knew him in the 1960s and before.

80
That's All Folks!

I've read many of them and most get it so, so wrong. They reflect the image; not the reality. As long as my marbles remain rolling, I have memories that are far more honest and genuine than those worthy tomes which do, understandably, reflect the media image and the conventional wisdom.

But the Bowie experience highlights one of the best aspects of my life. And something I have found enormously satisfying. Finding, nurturing and encouraging talent. Not always giant rock talent like Bowie or Genesis or 10cc. Not even just film or theatrical talent like The Rocky Horror Show. Not only pop like The Bay City Rollers or Who Let The Dogs Out or Abba or I Get Knocked Down (But I Get Up Again - my theme song for this dodgy century).

Spotting talent in every area of life and encouraging it. One friend, for whom I bought a refurbished computer, 35 years ago, as his family could not afford one, is now a top executive in a computer firm. Another, my coffee boy during the Brits, is now head of a huge Security firm. And incidentally looks after my very complicated and expensive home security - refusing to take a penny for it.

Dear Sir Edward Lewis, dying of cancer, told his wife "Jonathan is the only person I've ever met who never wanted anything from our friendship except friendship". In fact, on his deathbed, he wanted to give me his Decca

Record Company, as long as I promised to run it myself for the rest of my life. I refused, as I really did not enjoy being a "boss". He couldn't believe I turned down a gift worth 85 million quid. But then he did. All I wanted was friendship. And to break great music.

I could have made millions from David Bowie but I didn't want to. I just wanted to help him realise his talent. That was satisfaction enough.

80
That's All Folks!

Chapter 5

CRIMINAL CONVICTIONS; FALSE ACCUSERS; CASE STUDY ONE

And so we move away from a couple of famous fairies to real life liars…

It may be that the media is correct. Readers are more interested in celebrities, dead or alive, than in complicated and boring legal and criminal subjects. But recent events, like the horrifying events of the Post Office/Horizon scandal, have been turned into ENTERTAINMENT and have become hugely popular with viewers, fascinated by how broken the system has become. Globally, as well as just in the UK.

And my chosen career as a communicator was affected by legal interference often inspired by "political" reasons.

I've written elsewhere about how the strange turn in the road of my life took place in the year 2000. I had been offered and had accepted the job of Global Chairman of EMI Records at the salary, then, of £5 million a year for

80
That's All Folks!

a firm, guaranteed ten years.

Although I hated running companies and have just mentioned turning down Decca, it dawned on me that, by appointing good people to take care of all the boring stuff - share holders, human resources, taxes, financial and legal rubbish (God I hate lawyers) - I could probably quite enjoy saving the global music industry.

A key EMI executive in America or, rather, I gather, his wife, had contacted a friend of hers, the devious but bright publicist Max Clifford, and asked him if he could, in some way, stop this from happening, as they were well aware that my first decision would be to fire him and most of the other useless and expensive executives. EMI were notoriously bad in the vital American market.

Clifford had famously specialised in sex scandals, often involving famous footballers, frequently with women prepared to make false or exaggerated claims, and had branched out to include politicians like David Mellor and Neil Hamilton, being well aware that there were fortunes to be made in this area.

Whether true, false or even slightly true, and only needing exaggeration, there was cash in a good story and even more in a great story.

He remembered one false accuser, Kirk McIntyre, who had approached him about other people involved in the disco The Walton Hop. Clifford had sent him away with a flea in his ear, as the men accused were not famous enough to warrant any publicity or media fees. One of them was former BBC DJ Chris Denning, of whom more later.

Clifford then contacted McIntyre and asked whether he had ever met Jonathan King and whether, thinking about it, he might also have been abused by that celebrity.

Later, McIntyre **bravely waived his right to anonymity**, a strange law devoted to concealing the names of those claiming to be sex abuse victims, whether or not their allegations proved true or false. In return for a large sum of money McIntyre allowed photos, stories and even, in his case, film of him finally meeting me, for the first time, in a hotel lobby after I'd been released from prison, an event organised by, and captured by, The Sun.

"Insist on shaking his hand", they instructed him, "and don't let go until we've got a good photo of you "confronting" him".

So dodgy were the McIntyre allegations that they never came to court in 2001; they were revived in 2018 and I was acquitted of all his claims. Because of his brave waive, I can now, of course, include his name here.

And another false accuser, Christopher Sealey, was my main accuser in 2001, and his case is an interesting one, currently being reconsidered in 2025 by the CCRC.

I cite it and others in detail here, because it may benefit

80
That's All Folks!

others being accused in the future. And also because, hopefully, many police officers will be reading this and may realise how, in all conscience, liars can manipulate the system, sometimes from genuinely mistaken memory but sometimes also in order to make huge amounts of money.

Decent cops - I believe, the majority - really hate "what's going on", as one of the officers in 2001 said privately to my face, and subsequently left the force.

Chris Sealey, who later "bravely waived" his right to anonymity in return for several large sums, including a well paid interview on ITV in a morning show hosted by, amongst others, John Leslie - later, like Clifford, to become a victim of allegations.

Found GUILTY of his charges in 2001, I was sentenced to 7 years in prison for a crime that had never taken place. So, obviously, I foolishly thought, there could have been no evidence that it had.

I cannot remember how or why I met Sealey. Back in the 1970s and 1980s I used something called Word of Mouth to break records. I had a huge list of names and addresses of people who were willing to spread the word - give opinions on new releases, request them from radio stations, rave about them to DJs. I called them my **King's Army**. I sent them free, promotion copies of new singles or albums for their opinion and, if they liked them, asked them to tell friends and others about them. It was a hugely successful way of breaking hits, instead of the massive expense of promoting and marketing the tracks, and had the advantage of letting me know if something had real potential and commercial appeal or not.

The appalling 2001 Prosecutor David Jeremy asked me, in cross examination, "If it was so effective, why wasn't everybody else doing it?". I replied to his sneering question "I don't know - you'll have to ask them".

The King's Army was all genders, all ages and all races but predominantly teenagers. I met them in queues, at gigs, in clubs, on the street. I spoke to everyone. Remember, at the time I was a celebrity. Many approached me, asking for an autograph or simply praising a record of mine or a TV show. 99% were decent, polite, helpful and delighted to get involved.

Sometimes they visited my home - boys only - girls were too dangerous - even in those days, paternity suits were claimed against wealthy, famous men, if the spotty teenage boyfriend had failed to wear a contraceptive.

Listened to music, told about their lives and yes, sometimes, as long as they were over 16 and willing, we had sex.

I can only judge the first encounter with Sealey from his interview with the News of the World in 1997. Demanding £250,000 for his fictional tale of being

80
That's All Folks!

seduced by me in 1984/5, and rejected as fantasy by the newspaper then, he told journalist Sean O'Brien the following.

He had been on a trip to London with friends - Spanish boys who were staying with his family for a few weeks, through his mother's connection to the local church. He was with one friend, either in an arcade (I would never have visited one) or a record shop. When I had approached him, asked them both about music, gave them my phone number and left.

Then (Lie Number One) they went to Hamleys - a London shop - and they bought a set of cricket pads with money that "I had given them".

Why on earth would I have given them money? He later, in court documents, admitted he had lied about this, as he'd stolen the money from his mother's purse. He had made up a lot about meeting me in order to deflect attention from that.

What DID happen was that, a few weeks later he phoned me. Said he'd be in town again and could we meet up? Again I cannot remember the circumstances but I clearly did meet him, probably bought him a coffee or a Coca Cola, would likely have contributed to his travel expenses - £10 or so - given him some records, asked for opinions and left it at that.

I would have asked him to make sure it was OK with

his parents if I sent him some records. I would probably also have suggested that he shouldn't boast about knowing me, as that would affect any value he had, getting opinions on the music from friends. I later learned he had, indeed, boasted about meeting me, even telling his school friends that I'd paid for his cricket pads on that first occasion.

Over the next few years he came to London several times, visiting my home. I liked him. He was a bit of a villain, lying about everything, a chancer who once turned up, early one morning, with a friend from school in order for me to tell the friend that I had girlfriends and was not, in any way, sexually involved with Chris. I think he was being teased at school and needed evidence that I was a hot bloodied, heterosexual male.

He knew I was bisexual and he knew it was illegal for males to have sex with the same gender, if either was below 21. After he turned 16 he often used, jokingly, to request I give him a blow job. I, equally jokingly, refused.

Because he was becoming a pest. Several times a week he would phone me, asking if he could visit. On the few times he did visit, he asked for larger and larger sums "to cover his ticket down". So annoying were his calls that I had to change my phone number, putting my previous number onto a fax machine. And that seemed to work. We lost touch.

80
That's All Folks!

I never knew about the News of the World attempt. But when I was arrested some years later in 2000, he swiftly went to the police. Changing his story radically, and making it far more outrageous, after the rejection from the News of the World.

Surrey Police contacted Sean O'Brien who told them in detail about the attempt from years beforehand. On seeing the discrepancies, Surrey Police chose NOT to inform my defence team of anything other than the basic details of the attempt to extract money, which was, in itself, quite damaging to his claim.

But my team never knew the many and contradictory claims detailed in his original claim, until the transcript of the O'Brien interview was accidentally submitted to us, by mistake, in 2017, before the 2018 trial.

My new lawyers could not believe the differences and it was obvious why Surrey Police had deliberately, in 2001, failed to disclose it. Any jury would have acquitted me, hearing the contradictions. And, had the defence been shown the O'Brien transcript, they would have tracked down and brought to London the Spanish friend, to corroborate the original story.

The main difference was that Sealey, in his sworn police and Court statement, claimed he had been alone when he had met me outside a Peep Show in Soho and that I had taken him into a booth inside and then to my

JONATHAN KING

house, where the offence had occurred.

Apart from the contradictions between the News of the World detailed story and this adapted version years later, a decent defence team should have interviewed staff from the Peep Show, who would have sworn it would have been totally impossible for a major celebrity - myself in 1986 - to have entered the establishment, let alone with a teenage boy. And that it would have been physically impossible for two people to enter a tiny booth.

I've learned this over the subsequent years. In 2001 I assumed you did not hire a dog and bark yourself. My utterly useless defence team - QC Ronald Thwaites and solicitor Peter Hughman - failed me on several counts. But that was, and I think remains, par for the course. Most innocent victims of allegations rely on the efficiency of busy lawyers who have many cases and simply don't think about such obvious tasks as demanding undisclosed evidence.

A lot of other fresh evidence has emerged since - such as Sealey's friend, who had been dragged to my house, who also testified at the trial, now, in 2024, admitting Sealey tried to get him to change his story at the Old Bailey, which he refused to do. This kind of evidence alone, now obtained by a Private Investigator, would have got a trial stopped at the time. But the O'Brien interview with police is SO damaging to Sealey's story and is SO

80
That's All Folks!

certain to have affected the jury's decision that, in 2025, I am anticipating the conviction to be sent back to the Court of Appeal and the conviction quashed.

However, this depends on the CCRC.

The Criminal Cases Review Commission.

The CCRC has been seriously damaged by several cases this century - one of which concerned Andrew Malkinson, a man who served 17 years in prison for a rape he did not commit and which the CCRC should have sent back to the Court of Appeal years before they did. This was detailed by the Court of Appeal when they examined Malkinson's case and granted THREE of his five reasons - the first (DNA) being fresh evidence, but Grounds 2&3 (Police Failure to Disclose evidence) had been rejected by the CCRC years earlier and had not been sent to the Court of Appeal, as it should have been.

Similar to my own claims - and the respected journalist Bob Woffinden had included both Malkinson and my cases in his 2016 book about the **ten worst miscarriages of justice in the UK** over the previous 30 years. **The Nicholas Cases.** Andrew has one chapter. I have another.

The CCRC only refers a tiny amount of cases back to the Court. I suspect correctly, in many claims, but wrongly in many others. Under 2% referred back? Absurd. It should be at least 20-30% if not more. Underfunded as, I suspect, Government really doesn't want the system to be too closely examined, as the public would lose all faith in it. Which is happening more and more. Almost daily murders are found, thanks to DNA, not to have been committed by those convicted. This is terrifying.

Apart from anything else, it means there are hundreds of killers walking around free to commit more killings. But, worse, the implication is that thousands convicted of crimes where there can never be any DNA evidence, often because the crimes never took place, will never be exonerated.

I am one of those.

The Courts get many trials wrong. Partly because police, determined to get convictions, fail to examine or try to find evidence proving the innocence of the accused. Partly because most lawyers are useless. Mainly because the accused, as I was, rely on the professionals and the fairness of the system.

It made no sense to me that, if something never happened, I could be convicted of a crime I not only did not commit but that HAD NEVER HAPPENED. How could that occur in a fair and honest society?

"Just ask the Post Office sub postmasters" I can hear you shout.

I liked Chris Sealey, despite the fact that he was clearly destined for a life of crime and addiction. He made me

80
That's All Folks!

laugh. Even whilst he was at school he fibbed and invented fantasies. And, as he advanced from cigarettes, alcohol and cannabis - all before he met me - to heroin addiction, he became a pest who needed cash for his habit. I probably should NOT have dumped him for purely selfish reasons, but should have helped him, as a friend. So I do not consider myself blameless. Nor do I blame him. I don't even just blame the police ("doing their jobs") or the lawyers (they could not exist only having one client at a time). Nor the judge nor the jury (easily fooled and mainly concerned with problems such as what to have for dinner that night). Nor the media (it was a great story). I blame society which has not adapted.

Chris died young. A drug addict who mixed with very dodgy suppliers and dealers. Too late to be helped now.

When, in 2017, we found the transcript of O'Brien's interview with the police, we immediately notified the CCRC. It was obvious that this had never been shown, either to the defence nor the Court. The CCRC decided it HAD been disclosed, despite the fact that the hand written transcript was noted, on the cover sheet, that it had been typed and filed on the first of October 2001 by DC Loving, who still works for Surrey Police. The trial involving Sealey was in September. How on earth could the CCRC consider the vital evidence HAD been disclosed a month earlier?

JONATHAN KING

You would think, at least, they would have interviewed DC Loving to check that it was her note on the hand written original. Extraordinary inefficiency, laziness or deliberate avoidance of effort which could, indeed, indicate my innocence and the likelihood that the jury would have acquitted me. We are still protesting this wrong conclusion by the CCRC, eight years later. What's a girl to do?

But what I can do is write this down. Whether or not my wrongful convictions get overturned, this chapter and this book as a whole must surely alert victims of false allegations to the vital, crucial pieces of advice. Do everything yourself. Read every word of every single statement. Check all claims. Examine everybody's background. Do not rely on others.

If it happens to you, take total control of your defence. If you are innocent.

And if an independent body fails to perform basic functions, it may even be Attempting to Pervert the Course of Justice. The CCRC recently rejected applications of evidence by Jeremy Bamber in another (murder) case. He had proof that a cop had given sworn evidence to the New Yorker magazine about a vital phone call. But they did this without interviewing the police officer or the journalist or editor of the magazine. DOH!!!

80
That's All Folks!

Enablers. Those who encourage, collude, persuade and even tell how to adapt and inflate stories without technically lying. These are the real villains. Many lawyers and PR persons and even many cops.

One of my heroes is **CARL BEECH**. This imbecile spotted there was a fortune to be made by Using The Law To Break The Law. Especially naming dead people as sex abusers. He is just one of thousands.

He was supported by all the usual enablers including some who, since, have fallen from grace and been exposed as either abusers themselves or simply as liars. He cropped up on all the usual enabler sites - some of which genuinely tried to help those genuinely abused. The more he was accepted and encouraged, the wilder his accusations became. Starting with dead people, especially high profile dead people, like ex Prime Minister and closet gay Sir Edward Heath, his tales expanded, encouraged by enablers.

As Keir Starmer - then Director of Public Prosecutions, had once advised police and liars - "You will be believed". No qualifications. Which, by default, meant "even if you are lying". And "even if you want to make a lot of money".

And Beech did. His stories began to include living people. Why not? Trawling through past cuttings, as the Internet archive is SOO valuable to false accusers and their enablers, he came up with past gays or celebrities and even accused them of murder. Bodies need not be found (there weren't any).

Proof and evidence no longer mattered. An allegation was enough. He banked the cash. Bought an expensive car. Travelled. Paid rent boys. Lived the life. He was SOO stupid but convinced, and why wouldn't he be?, that he was untouchable. He really didn't bother to check the accuracy of his dates. Why would he - my 2001 case, amongst others, had shown that dates could be changed during a trial, on a whim, without any time given for the accused to find fresh alibis?.

Lazy or bent cops, encouraged by the DPP and others, went along with it. Promotion loomed. Increased budgets. And, best of all, massive media praise and coverage.

It all collapsed. As was inevitable. And that's why he's a hero of mine. By being stupid, and daring to test the limits of the system, he brought attention to a situation that everybody chose to ignore. He's currently serving 18 years for his trouble when actually he should have been awarded a medal.

Yet society and most of the media STILL continues to ignore it.

As I type this Lady Diana Brittan, the widow of Sir Leon Brittan, one of the many falsely accused who died before he was cleared, has exploded on the BBC. She's furious that the IOPC, one of the toothless watchdog

80
That's All Folks!

quangos like the CCRC, which took over from the IPPC (see elsewhere and in other volumes) has decided to drop its investigation into the Beech situation.

Now I may have misconstrued this, in which case please forgive me and do not sue, the IOPC has found that serving police officers are far more efficient than the IOPC at "finding" missing E-Mails and indeed at "losing" E-Mails and, as a result, there is "no case to answer". I think that was what they said.

Lady Brittan on Radio Four said "My husband was a high-profile individual, but at every level of society there are people who are falsely accused, and for them (also) it's the ruining of reputation, it's the anxiety that goes with it. I feel that it would have at least put a closure, to use that odd word, on the whole episode if somebody had been held to account, either for misconduct, or even for incompetence."

Do I blame the IOPC? No, no, no.

Like the CCRC, underfunded, running with a Government agenda ("wink wink; nudge nudge; NEVER find against a serving cop/sitting Judge"), tiny budget, useless staff, without a clue about what is going on...

Elsewhere I discuss the Milly Dowler case, the Deepcut Barracks case... often involving Surrey Police. But the public doesn't care. Why would it?

It's not "a good story".

JONATHAN KING

Chapter 6

MARGARET THATCHER, THE BRITS, TOP OF THE POPS AND YET MORE EUROVISION

As a young lad I found it difficult to understand when politicians or journalists called Prime Minister Margaret Thatcher attractive. Then I met her and understood. Not sexually attractive, not even physically attractive, but enormously attractive emotionally and intellectually.

I disagreed with many of her policies socially, though I felt her basic economic approach was sound. In my opinion society depends on a few entrepreneurs who have to be socially responsible and honourable.
Those make the fortunes which enables those in need to be looked after. Bill Gates is a great example - giving away most of his millions to deserving charities and people in need. Bruce Springsteen, The Boss, is another.

I'm a bit odd like that. A capitalist who agrees with many of the Communist aspirations. Where I am very different is that I do not agree with Democracy -

80
That's All Folks!

particularly since the media grew all powerful, with the vast majority believing almost every word printed, picture shown or statement heard.

Thatcher and Blair had much in common - realising that image is everything. You can sell anything to the voters, if the sales pitch is done correctly. Stifle or, better, mock opposition.

I first encountered her in person when I was producing The Brits. I interviewed her in No10 Downing Street and, at one point, asked her which was her favourite song. "How Much Is That Doggy In The Window?", she replied.

"How does that go?", I asked, knowing full well.

She twinkled at me. She knew exactly what I wanted, considered whether or not it would be damaging to give it to me, decided to assist me and slowly crooned…

"How much is that doggy in the window - the one with the waggly tail?".

I still regard that moment, captured on film, as my greatest ever achievement, and it was totally down to her. She knew it was risky, she knew it would be great television, she liked me and trusted I would not use it against her.

The audience at the live Brits were totally silent, then gasped, then applauded like crazy. It was one of those moments.

Later Ben Elton, the satirist, who I really like, rang to ask me if he could use the footage in a sketch he was planning. I declined.

"Much though I love your shows, I am not willing to provide you with bullets", I said.

When I arrived to do the interview at No 10, she looked at my colourful, hand painted waistcoat and said "What an interesting waistcoat. Where did you get it?".

"Harrods, Prime Minister", I answered.

"Was it on sale?".

I collapsed in laughter.

"You're not meant to have a sense of humour, Thatcher", I said. She smiled.

Indeed, on the several subsequent times I met her, I found she did indeed have a wicked sense of humour, sometimes expressed without words. I was cornered at a Downing Street event by Kenneth Baker - a Minister depicted as a slug with slime by Spitting Image. Sipping warm champagne and nibbling stale canapes, he was very nicely flattering me by saying how brilliant my records were. I caught Maggie's eyes across the room. She raised them to the sky. Again, I exploded with laughter.

She was funny, bright, and a very good listener. I constantly disagreed with her policies and told her why, in detail; sometimes she agreed, usually she disagreed. She was a very nice, very articulate woman. Quite petite with

80
That's All Folks!

perfect skin. In many ways I regret we didn't become closer friends - we were both very busy.

I rather suspect she wanted her daughter Carol to marry me. Carol was well aware of my inclinations and knew this was never on the cards. Another very nice lady and a very good broadcaster.

Anyway, after saving The Brits in the early 1990s - a story told in greater detail elsewhere - my reputation for being rather good behind the scenes was growing. And the BBC appointed a new Head of Light Entertainment - a man called David Liddiment who I'd never met but who was based in Manchester.

I was due to be in the city, as the star interview at In The City, a music convention, and contacted Liddiment to ask if we could meet for breakfast, which we did.

My sole reason was to persuade him to allow me to take over Top of the Pops as Producer.

My dear show, that I had loved from Day One, as did virtually every UK teenager, and on which I had been a very early guest - on the very first London show; it had started in Manchester - in 1965. I had continued on it many times after that, including, in the 1980s, doing regular reports on the US music scene from my home in New York.

I felt responsible for the decline of the show, and thought I knew how to reverse it.

JONATHAN KING

Back in the 1970s I had decided that the show - hugely popular - was a key ingredient to breaking releases. The trouble was - the format predominantly used tracks which were on the charts and climbing. So I needed to get my releases onto the charts.

This was done through contacting retailers who supplied their weekly returns to the chart company, and persuading them to sell lots of copies of my releases. It came to be called Chart Hype later, but it really wasn't. It was just getting retailers involved as part of my King's Army.

This was not hard. I was a very big star at the time and a call or visit from me impressed local retailers. Quite apart from anything else, it attracted positive attention when a Rolls Royce arrived at their shop. One Saturday I managed to visit 65 shops in one day. Every one subsequently sold half a dozen copies that day - and reported that to the chart compilers.

But far more important was the fact that, thanks to The King's Army - my battalion of helpers around the country, who not only spread the word but let me know whether the promotion releases were genuinely liable to become popular or not - I only ever pushed or "hyped" future smashes. Because that not only stopped me from pushing flops, and wasting precious funds doing that, but gave me a reputation for being right about future hits.

80
That's All Folks!

So retailers were delighted to go further than for other releases, and actively pushed my product. "Listen to this". "This is going to be big". They got great reputations with their customers for predicting hits way ahead of the charts.

They then reported the sales in their diaries, which was how charts were compiled back then - and remember, only a few hundred shops carried or sold singles outside the Top 50. The diaries were collected by the chart compiler organisations.

The releases charted. And went on Top of the Pops. And exploded, because they were potentially real hits. It was through this method that I beat the other version by George Baker of Una Paloma Blanca in 1975, with my record reaching the Top 5 whilst his only made the Top 10.

The snag was… the big labels spotted my trick and soon started doing the same, only more so - offering gold watches and bottles of champagne in return for fake ticks in the diaries and - this was the real problem - they did it on their priority releases, many of which had no commercial appeal at all, but were by artistes that had cost a lot to sign and promote, or were by the CEO's wife and so on.

The result? Quickly the chart no longer reflected music of true, cross over, mass appeal. Viewers started noticing this - by the 1980s, Top of the Pops featured record after record that nobody liked. Ratings dipped, shrank, disappeared.

The TV show was dying. I knew why and I thought I knew how to solve it.

Put someone in charge (me) who could hear or see real mass appeal and would refuse to show tracks hyped into the top 5 if they weren't actually any good. Who could not be bought (me - the only thing I cared about was the music and the show).

I liked Liddiment immediately. He turned out to love music too and actually turned me onto an unknown group, I'd never heard of, called Chumbawamba - more of that elsewhere and later. He liked me too. He agreed - yes I could take over the Pops, after he'd investigated the situation of the series and could I please also take over Eurovision - a disaster in the ratings with the channel controller, Alan Yentob, on the verge of cancelling it.

Sadly, David discovered that his predecessor had pledged and signed a Radio One radio producer to take over Top of the Pops. Ric Blaxill, a nice enough young man who, I knew, would not be able to save the show - as indeed he didn't.

But would I please, PLEASE, take over Eurovision. I sighed and agreed.

The reason I was hesitant was because I had never

80
That's All Folks!

liked Eurovision. As I've mentioned earlier. And there is quite a lot I didn't cover in the chapter beforehand. Despite the fact that one of the acts we published in our group of companies had won Eurovision - ABBA - and we published them through Bocu Music because their manager Stig Anderson had watched my success in England in the 60s and early 70s and wanted my involvement. All I ever did, in reality, was hear the demos and select the singles - in my opinion.

I'd been a fan of the odd entry - I hate to repeat myself but Are You Sure by The Allisons in 1961 UK came second. Non Ho L'Eta by Gigliola Cinquetti for Italy won in 1964, and I'd not mentioned Love Is Blue by Paul Mauriat in 1967 for Luxembourg, though not this version. But generally the songs and the acts were crap.

So, I thought, find a hit song and we'll win.

Easier said than done. The first year I found a great track - Love City Groove, by a mixed race band of the same name, which became a Top Ten hit as well as being the most played track on KISS-FM, a pirate station at the time, loved by the young and by the rap/hip hop community - thus achieving my goal of attracting a whole new audience to Eurovision.

The problem was - the EBU still, back then, insisted on acts performing live, with an orchestra. This was NOT the way music was made in 1995. New techniques in recording, writing and arranging had not been reflected in Eurovision. I felt they HAD to be and managed to persuade the EBU to alter the rules for future years and to allow backing tracks. A major breakthrough - but no help to me in 1995. We came 10th. Still, a good showing. A chart breakthrough. A new audience.

Yentob was furious. Eurovision was saved. Big ratings increase. He tore me off a strip in a BBC corridor. But he could no longer cancel it. I'm sorry if it seems like I'm repeating myself but this gives an insight into other areas of music than my previous Eurovision centred chapter.

So for the next year I got the best music people involved. Liddiment had moved up to being boss of ITV but had been replaced by Mike Leggo at the BBC, an old friend who had started off as a junior researcher on my Entertainment USA series. So I continued.

My deal with the BBC was a strange one, except to those who knew me. Expenses only but a massive bonus if (when) we won.

One friend, Steve Long, had a girlfriend at the time, an Australian lady who worked behind the checkout counter at Woolworths in Hampstead. I didn't know or really believe there WAS a Woolworths in Hampstead - very much an Marks and Spencer or Waitrose area of London.

Working with bright new young producers and my friend Rob Dickins at Warners, they came up with Ooh

80
That's All Folks!

Aah Just A Little Bit which I felt was the perfect Eurovision entry and, as I've said before, I still do - to this day.

Astonishingly we totally failed to win The Eurovision Song Contest. In fact we came 8th. I despaired. I remember meeting Rob in Oslo and saying "If I can't win with that, I might as well give up". He was very supportive, pointing out the track was No1 all around the world including the UK and had even become a hit in America, selling more copies than almost every other Eurovision hit over the decades.

But I knew I couldn't top that. I quit.

Mike Leggo went ballistic.

"We've never had higher viewing figures. It's one of the Most Watched BBC shows this year. It's been a huge ratings hit - totally thanks to you with a foot in both camps - TV and Music. Please, please, PLEASE stay on. Give it at least one last try".

So I did. I worked out that Gina G, a sweet girl, was not a real performer and there needed to be a hard sell, visually. So we settled on Katrina - who I'd known from years before, when I'd championed a track she had, called Walking On Sunshine - written by Kimberly Rew, who had put together an anthemic chant called Love Shine A Light.

It was perfect. To repeat - still the most TWELVE

JONATHAN KING

POINTS (douze points) in ratio to amount of countries voting - ever. It won. Katrina giggled that there were more shots of me waving the flag, which I still have on my mantelpiece at home, than there were of her during the voting. She was brilliant - really selling the song, although I still think Just A Little Bit was the best of all my entries.

I did manage to enter, into the UK contest, Yodel In The Canyon Of Love, a song about female sexuality sung by a super girl Kelly, who was disabled from the waist down. I regard that as a triumph on several fronts.

Mike Leggo was over the moon. "I think I love you JK", he said, hugging me. We hosted the show in the next year in Birmingham. That year we came second with Imaani. What japes!

A few years later I put together another dead cert winner - I thought. Again written by Kimberley Rew, we found six girls, all from different decades, from the teens up to the 60s. Called them Six Chix. Kim wrote a song for them called Only The Women Know. Another real hit. Very exciting.

But I felt morally obliged to let the BBC know of my involvement in putting them together - as Executive Producer, it would be unfair if I was involved in the actual final selection process. So I technically resigned from that part of the structure - after four finalists had been chosen, I would sit to one side until an entrant was chosen;

80
That's All Folks!

divorcing myself from the public vote and count; then return, to steer whoever won into the actual Eurovision show.

This was fine with the BBC, which felt it covered any accusations of cronyism. Sadly though, and this is only my suspicion, they feared that my connection to the Six Chix project would damage the credibility of the choice. So, to my astonishment, Six Chix were announced as SECOND and the winner was Nikki French with a dreadful, no hope song, appropriately called Don't Play That Song Again. That was the end of the UK's chances that year and, as it turned out, forever, including 2025.

Tragic, sad and spelled the end of my time running the BBC end of the show. Although I puttered on for a couple more years, my heart was no longer in it.

As it happened, David Liddiment, over at ITV, gave me an annual slot for my Tipsheet Record of the Year show, which got huge ratings every Christmas and boosted music sales phenomenally each year.

And in 2025 a sad fact emerged, which I have not mentioned before. Rather as the music industry in the 1970s, impressed by my way of breaking potential future hits by getting them charted and on TV, ruined the concept by doing it with all their awful priorities, devoting vast sums, plus gold watches and champagne bottles, to hyping rubbish and thus wrecking the whole industry, so it happened with televoting.

My idea had been to involve the public, instead of just relying on my own ears - it started with the UK contest on radio with my dear friend and supporter Terry Wogan, on the BBC and Radio Two. I then persuaded the EBU to incorporate it into the actual Eurovision shows. OK, I was pretty good at finding hits but if the British public chose a song that was potentially a bigger hit, that should be the UK entry. And the television audience for Eurovision would probably be a better judge of commerciality than panels of self regarding judges.

But a combination of media hype and cunning use of hype as with Israel in 2025, which fortunately didn't quite work with their crap entry that came second to Austria - also crap but slightly better crap.

If Israel's use of manipulating media fails similarly in Gaza and the West Bank, we should see peace and justice come to the region sooner rather than later; a UN supported recognition of Palestine as a country and the end to mindless stupid killing on both sides, with internationally protected borders and security from terrorists. Who, let's be honest, are also good at media manipulation.

I only hope the EBU gets sense put back into the voting process and the music industry starts putting forward decent, mass appeal songs into the contest.

80
That's All Folks!

JONATHAN KING

Chapter 7

MORE CASE HISTORIES FROM 2001

I've explained my main wrongful conviction in 2001, that of Christopher Sealey, in an entire different chapter. But the remaining complainants and convictions deserve further coverage here. I've not gone into them before, because there was need for further investigation and also because some of them did not "bravely waive their anonymity" in return for large sums of cash from tabloid newspapers.

It's a very strange rule that, if someone lies or exaggerates, making claims of sex abuse, historical or recent, and is found to have been mistaken at best or lying at worst, they are legally allowed to remain anonymous for life.

This law MUST be changed. It allows extortion, blackmail, perverting the course of justice, perjury and many other crimes, which are rarely if ever prosecuted. False claimants and criminals like Carl Beech and Jemma

80
That's All Folks!

Beale are just the tips of the iceberg.

Sometimes false accusers genuinely believe their stories. Often the passing of years, and the effect of media coverage of other cases, convinces them that their memories are absolutely correct, but it is frequently the case that there is a load of evidence there proving them false, if only someone can find it. A great story produces dozens of copycat claims - sometimes as many as 50 or 100, or many more if the victim is dead and cannot fight back.

Every day now there's a story about someone, usually wealthy and famous, who has crossed the line of acceptable behaviour. Not just serious abuse or exaggerated encounters but simple words or actions that might offend. People are so easily offended this century.

First - an apology. It must bore the pants off readers to hear details of unimportant, trivial claims and often we, the victims, take offence at the wrong things. It was 25 years ago that this happened to me but many more, in 2025, are suffering claims this century, as I predicted they would. A gold mine has been opened and prospectors are piling into the seam of wealth.

My friend Paul Gambaccini, who was persecuted, like me, for crimes that never took place, phoned me daily at the time with complaints about police activity. At one point they had contacted the parents of two of his godsons. This, as you will understand, caused distress. But, as I pointed out to Gambo - this is fair enough police procedure.

Much, however, is not. Some is actually criminal behaviour by police, which has recently emerged as bent cops killed and raped people using their Warrant Cards as a weapon.

TRIAL OFFENCE ONE...
At trial we, the defence, managed to prove the dates on several of the claims were impossible. So the CPS applied, during the trial, for permission to change the dates. After the false accusers had been cross examined. Their request was granted. But when we applied to have time to find alternative alibis for the new dates which were always later, making the complainants older, we were REFUSED permission to do so. Why? Surely that is terribly unfair?

My expensive lawyers said it was "standard legal procedure". I said that did not make it fair or right. They looked at me as though I was mad. They also assured me that HHJ Paget, the trial judge, would make clear the disadvantages to me in his summing up. He did not. All he said was that, because the time frames were so broad, I could not say something like "I was in America" at the time.

But in one case I could and did - years later - find

80
That's All Folks!

exactly that, as the new time frame was a mere three days and, if I had been allowed a few days to investigate, I would have found solid, rock hard alibis.

One liar in particular had approached me in a supermarket where he was with his parents on one of their regular, annual trips to London, saying he loved my show NO LIMITS. We proved it had not been made or broadcast until over a year later, making him 14 and not 13.

Then, subsequently, we proved it could not have been then either, and the Court had to wait until his mother's diary had been fetched and brought to court and it showed it was, again, a year later that he first might have met me, according to his mother's rather confused entry, making him 15 not 14.

After I was released from jail I found I had been in America over his latest dates - from September 6th to 9th 1985 - with loads of proof, passport stamps, air tickets - I often flew Concorde or Pan Am, witness statements and so on. We presented this to the CCRC. Had the dates been altered for another time - a year later he would have been 16.

The CCRC said it was not **WHEN** something happened but **WHETHER**. In a case concerning the Age of Consent when, by then, it was legal over 16. DOH!!!!!

JONATHAN KING

I remember seeing the final indictment, put to the jury, after my release, and finding it extraordinary that, instead of changing the dates clearly and reprinting the indictment, they were simply scribbled out, with new dates often almost illegible and numerous errors, like failing to change some of the ages so a 13 year old, on those new dates, is still listed as 13 and not 15.

Just to clarify - the words presented to the Jury to consider a verdict were "On a day between the 6th day of September 1985 and the 9th day of September 1985 attempted to commit buggery with XX, a male person under the age of 21, being 13 years".

But he wouldn't have been 13. He would have been 15. A jury might well have considered such an offence against a 13 year old to be far more serious than against a 15 year old. They might have thought, after the age had been changed twice, that a third time was pushing it. They might not have noticed some of these changes, since the age on the indictment remained the same despite the date changes - perhaps they should have done and should have requested clarity from the Judge, but they didn't. Perhaps HHJ Paget should have noticed and demanded a correction. He didn't.

So I was found guilty of a charge which was impossible. British justice?

I committed a crime in London, according to the jury,

80
That's All Folks!

when I was in America against a boy of 13 who was actually 15 on those dates. And the CCRC, instead of sending it back to the Court of Appeal to consider, said it was not **when** a (totally consensual, according to the accuser) crime was committed, but **whether** it happened, that the jury had decided.

Ah, the CCRC will say, but someone of 13 cannot consent to sex, so it was still a crime. But he wasn't 13 - he was 15, according to the law. And might have been 16 if we'd been allowed to find the evidence we found years later.

Alice is alive and well in Wonderland, in front of the Red Queen. Off with her head.

In reality, I never had any kind of sex with the fan. That was probably one reason he kept coming back.

In what world can such a thing happen, one asks? In dictatorships? Yes - expected. Enemies of the State - and I am certainly one of them. We can and indeed should be locked up. In Communist countries and places where the ruling administration demands total control over everything - check out the superb Brazilian film I'm Still Here. In those territories still under the thumb of strict, powerful monarchies - do any exist in 2025?

I'm not a supporter of Democracy. It seldom works. Especially with media and the new social media, people vote on image. On stories. On photos. You get leaders with good teeth and nice hair, not with any ability.

But Great Britain is meant to be a fair and just democracy, where rules are obeyed. It is simply totally unfair for someone to face charges without being allowed a single second to discover a watertight alibi.

Over to Government. Over to Judges. I tell stories in other tomes about the Judges involved in my cases. Over to you, gentle reader.

TRIAL OFFENCE TWO...
One of the Claimants said he'd been brought round to my house when he was 12 by his older brother, had come several times after that and had, on the last of the subsequent occasions realised "what I was after" as I'd put my hand on his knee. He'd rushed off, never to see me again.

This was another of the "changed dates" claims on the indictment, though his age WAS changed from 12 to 15 and should have been "15 or 16" as the photo he produced as evidence, that he said I had given him on his first visit, had not been taken until he was almost 16, as we proved in court. It was a photo of me and Samantha Fox on her tour of America and her assistant gave evidence of the exact date and year that she had taken the photo.

The CPS admitted he could have been 16 after time taken for the photo to be processed and copies to be

80
That's All Folks!

made. But said it didn't matter, as CONSENT was an issue - all the others had admitted consent, as they had subsequently visited me on many occasions. He had not consented to a hand on his knee.

The two delightful pictures of myself and Sam Fox in Florida, very flattering to both of us and given to many fans, were indeed pics I handed out. I had no memory at all of ever having met this man, who now worked in a bank.

Nor of his older brother who, the man told police, was now gay, had no problems with me and did not want to be interviewed or to give evidence. That man - Andrew - who needs no anonymity - had no problem with me whatsoever.

You would have thought that my defence team would have asked for his contact details, would have interviewed him, would have discovered his brother had not been 12 but "15 or 16", if he had ever been taken to visit me, and would have revealed this at trial.

Just another example that not only are prosecution lawyers and police often useless or even corrupt, but ditto defence lawyers.

You don't hire a dog and bark yourself. Woof Woof.

My defence team cost me a million pounds and could neither bark nor bite nor, it seems, think. A lot of this I only found out in 2018 when "Unused Material", as it is called, was given to me for another, failed case - see later.

Police did NOT interview Andrew - taking his brother's word for it. Of course his brother did not want him interviewed - Andrew would have told them that his brother had been 15 or 16, as we later proved and he then had to admit, in court.

Police DID interview Andrew in 2018 over another matter - which was how I found out about the 2001 subterfuge. Can you imagine police NOT wanting to speak to the man who, allegedly, took his brother to meet me? It should have been essential evidence for the prosecution.

As I've said, I remember nothing about ever meeting this false accuser. So, if I never met him, how did he have the two photos of me with Sam Fox? After the 2018 fiasco, at which trial I was acquitted of all claims and any future retrial was banned, Surrey Police finally returned all my property from both the 2015/16 series of raids and, more importantly, from the 2001 raid.

Amongst these was a pack of photos - containing fresh copies I'd had made of the two pictures of me and Sam, taken in Florida by her assistant Paula, who had bravely come to court to give evidence about them.

So popular were the snaps that I'd had a dozen more of each printed up, after the first batch ran out, to give to fans. But they had stayed unopened, sealed, in a drawer

80
That's All Folks!

in my house. I'd never gotten around to opening them or giving them out. They had been seized and, I presumed, opened by police.

I even knew which officer, because documentation told me, when they were returned to me in late 2018. In the then unsealed same envelope from Snappy Snaps.

In which were 11 copies of each snap. 22 in total. Not 24.

I reckon a bent cop "supplied" the two photos to the claimant, produced "as evidence" during the trial and shown as having been given, by me, to this "12 year old" when I first met him. He'd not been able to ("lost them") produce them when first interviewed by Surrey Police and then ("found them") did so later.

Perhaps the helpful, friendly bent cop, now running a B&B on the South Coast, managed to "find" them for him. Without being aware that they proved he would have been "15 or 16" when he first met me - he claimed, let alone months later when I "tried it on" by putting a hand on his knee, causing him to rush out and never see me again.

Until in court, in 2001, by which time he was a bank employee and I was a Vile Pervert. You'll be pleased to hear that, after my trial and conviction, he applied for and received several thousand quid from the Criminal Injuries Compensation Board which, I hope, he banked with his own establishment.

A lot of this stuff goes on. Even WENT on, 25 years ago.

Good luck to them. Petty crooks supported by bent cops and a broken legal system. Hey I'm 80. What do I care?

Let me be clear; it is perfectly possible this man did visit me several times in his middle teens. It is perfectly possible, as he said, that all we did was listen to music and talk about music. It is perfectly possible that, after he became 16, I may have laid a hand on his knee and suggested a physical, sexual encounter.

What is impossible is that I suggested any such thing **before** he was 16. Which, incidentally, would still have been illegal, then, but I considered it ridiculous, since heterosexuality was legal from the age of 16.

TRIAL OFFENCE THREE...
One of Chris Sealey's friends, as I mentioned elsewhere, also gave evidence that I had indeed hosted him at my house.

This turned out to be, as we later learned, in order to prove to all Sealey's school friends that I was NOT a gay pervert but that I had dozens of girlfriends and a perfectly normal sex life - for a pop star.

I employed a superb Private Investigator - William

80
That's All Folks!

Merritt - who is mentioned elsewhere and did a brilliant job finding evidence that got me acquitted in 2018. I took him on, a couple of years ago, to track down Sealey's mother to find out whether she still had contact with the Spanish boy that her son had been with, when they first met me in London. At the same time I suggested he contacted the friend - SQ - who had given evidence and is therefore not entitled to anonymity, as he was not a "victim", but I feel he should not be named.

The mother was not helpful, as she did not any longer have contact with the Spanish boy. She would have had in 1985, as police well knew. But SQ was very helpful, though keen not to provide any evidence that might get my conviction quashed. He repeated his evidence exactly as delivered in court at trial. He said he was not prepared to alter a word and indeed had refused to do so when Sealey had tried to persuade him to do so in the Old Bailey "Victims Room" in 2001.

This is, of course, dynamite.

There were other "victims" in the room, either having given or being about to give evidence at the trial. Sealey might well have spoken to them and might also have tried to influence them - indeed, he had done so, according to his earlier admission to another Private Investigator years earlier. Read all about it in Bob Woffinden's excellent 2016 book The Nicholas Cases.

"Everyone was saying it, so I thought I might also" exaggerate the claims.

Had the Judge - HHJ Paget - been informed of this, he would certainly have stopped the trial.

TRIAL OFFENCE FOUR...
This involves someone who wasn't in my first 2001 trial. My defence team had persuaded HHJ Paget, in Legal Argument before the start of the actual trial, to divide it up into FOUR trials, making it easier to handle.

The original whistle blower, connected to PR person Max Clifford, was placed in Trial Four, to the delight of the prosecution, who were very aware of the flakiness of his evidence and claims. That liar was Kirk McIntyre, who I can name because... he bravely waived his anonymity so he could sell his story, with photographs, to the Sun, as detailed elsewhere.

McIntyre's claims were resurrected for my 2018 trial and were thrown out by HHJ Taylor at that point, who instructed the Jury to declare me Not Guilty of his charges, which they did.

Had my defence team in 2001 known all the evidence against McIntyre found by police, who failed to disclose it at the time, they would have insisted that McIntyre was included in the first trial as he was the "whistle blower" or first accuser in 2000. That would have brought the

80
That's All Folks!

number of accusers in Trial One up to SIX, a perfectly handleable amount.

And on hearing all the evidence proving McIntyre a liar, the jury would have been all the more likely to acquit me of ALL charges in that first trial. One of the pieces of fresh evidence was the list of asylums and rehab drug institutions he had attended before the year 2000, in which he had never mentioned my name, despite having named dozens of his abusers.

The CCRC say "Ah, but he wasn't part of Trial One and your convictions at that trial, so he cannot be used to quash them". We say that the failure to disclose evidence about him before the legal arguments affected the defence decision to leave him out of the first trial, and thus affected that procedure.

Trial Two in 2001 resulted in acquittal, so the CPS decided to abandon Trials Three and Four. Some of those claims were revived for the 2018 trial and failed dismally. I was then acquitted in 2018, after the trial collapsed, and one of the main reasons for that was the evidence against Kirk McIntyre.

TRIAL OFFENCE FIVE...
I go into much greater detail in my film **Vile Pervert The Musical** regarding the tricks police used back in 2001. Interviews were not video'd then; only recorded on audio

tape - remember those clips in movies of cops pressing buttons before introducing themselves?

So it was perfectly easy for a police officer to ask, on tape, "Was he circumcised?" - nod; thumbs up - "or uncircumcised?" shakes head; thumbs down. Even the thickest "witness" or "victim" could go along with this, often through information provided either by the reports of officers or from people who had legitimately experienced relationships and often refused to press charges but who had innocently divulged personal details.

"Do you remember what colour his Front Door was?" - waves blue tie. "It was blue". It was indeed - painted 20 years AFTER the claimed offence, at which point it had been white, as we brought the painter in to testify. Of course, search officers, a few months earlier, might have noticed it was blue as they broke it down, without realising how recently it had become that colour.

There were my "seduction packs" which, as shown in court, were the leather envelopes given on Concorde to all passengers - I'd collected dozens of them on my many flights.

And not just police behaviour but that of lawyers too; not only the prosecutors but my own incompetent defence team providing "inadequate representation at trial". As I've said elsewhere - not always their fault; they have many cases running at the same time. We assume

80
That's All Folks!

they are on top of every detail. They are not. They have neither the time nor the inclination nor the specific knowledge that only both parties can have.

Remember that the "victim" is supported by giant teams of hard working, though often stupid, cops and lawyers. The defendant has nobody except, often, legal aid lawyers. I spent a million quid on useless lawyers in 2001. In 2018 I was on legal aid, but fortunately with excellent lawyers, a decent judge, a great Private Investigator and had, over about 20 years, learned a lot. Do it yourself.

So we've seen that most police officers are perfectly decent, obeying orders, following instructions from above and told that, even if they wanted to, they should not be balanced and should simply find evidence that would, in court, get a conviction. We've seen lawyers, many working hard, many dedicated and honest, but all overworked and simply unable to cope with the vital areas of detail yet neither willing nor capable of telling clients they simply do not have the time nor the knowledge nor investigative powers to do a proper job. And Judges? Jurors?

Who wants be a juror? Far too complex to understand. Far too great a responsibility - either letting a dangerous criminal off, due to a technicality they don't comprehend, or sending an innocent person to jail through instinct or persuasion.

Sir Brian Leveson has just published an excellent report on reforming court procedure. He says that times have changed and the system needs to adapt to keep up with the changes. Spot on - as in much of life in this century.

Democracy was fine when it started. Not any more. The jury system worked OK, generally, in years gone by. Not any longer.

I've had two judges, essentially. Oh there were others during the course of all the trials and appeals, most notably the one in charge of a panel of three who understandably decided not to inform his fellow judges that he had known me at Cambridge and that we had had sex together.

It was illegal at the time in 1963 or 1964.

HHJ Paget - in 2001 - was awful. At the time he seemed fair, I thought, as an uninformed innocent. In hindsight, appalling. HHJ Taylor in 2018 was fantastic. Oh I would say that - acquitted, found Not Guilty on her instruction and any retrials forbidden. I hated her to start with, convinced she simply wanted me banged up. But, as she saw the evidence, heard the testimony of false accusers, spotted the flaws in the prosecution, she turned out to be that rare creature - a really good Judge. Sadly she is no longer a Judge, and I fear there are very few like

80
That's All Folks!

her remaining.

I have, of course, provided all of this evidence, both in the past and in the present, to the CCRC - more of them later. But one of their tricks to avoid having to spend time examining fresh evidence is to accuse the applicant (me) of being "vexatious". Of annoying their Case Manager with too many pieces of correspondence. Because he or she is "too busy" to be able to read and consider the odd letter.

They are working hard, they say, to reach a conclusion. And 25 years is not enough time for this complex investigation.

DOH!

Chapter 8

SEX WITH JOHN LENNON; THE BEATLES AND BRIAN EPSTEIN

I've gone into detail elsewhere about my friendship with John Lennon but don't seem to have covered our one and only sexual exploit. Plus not really enough about my - our - involvement with Yoko Ono. John was a very bright, witty and intelligent man, with a giant chip on his shoulder. He could be incredibly rude to people, though he never, ever was to me. In fact several times he would be tearing somebody off a strip and, if I was with him, then apologise to me afterwards.

Funny and great company except he took SOO many drugs and I didn't. He never tried to turn me on. The other non druggies in our 60s set were his lovely wife Cynthia, and Paul McCartney's girlfriend at the time, Jane Asher.

The three of us would end up at tables in clubs like the Scotch of St James drinking milk, in my case, and

80
That's All Folks!

wondering what on earth our friends had taken that day.

John and I would discuss everything - most of all music. I've described elsewhere how we would play tracks we loved again and again and then write a song that used a couple of the bits we really liked in a totally different setting. The trick was that nobody would ever spot where we'd taken the inspiration from. I remember my greatest success in that was from the Betty Wright US hit Clean Up Woman; and developing a similar but totally different riff into my It's A Tall Order For A Short Guy.

John loved that track. Only he and I ever knew the story behind it - until now.

The day after my very first Good Evening TV show had ended with me having slipped on the dry ice, studio floor coming out of the tent (don't ask) after interviewing my guest Yoko One who had been mind dancing (really, don't ask) - ending up flat on my back and having to sign off to millions of hysterical ITV viewers from a supine position on the floor, John spent the entire evening in a club grilling me about Yoko.

I told him I didn't like her husband at all - Tony Cox, an American. Her little daughter was sweet. Yoko too was sweet and bonkers, but I couldn't understand John's obsession - Cynthia was far lovelier.

I was actually rather annoyed during our conversation and snapped at him "What about the rest of the show?".

It was, after all, my virgin attempt at a Prime Time show on national television - ITV.

"Great. I loved it. You were great. But tell me more about this Ono woman…"

I need to say this to put the record straight. So many biographies are written about celebrities and others without asking some of those who knew them such as staff, friends, and even passing acquaintances. The conventional wisdom is that Yoko was a predator - the woman "who broke up The Beatles", the Japanese frump who set out to seduce and win the wealthy superstar Lennon. This is absolutely untrue.

John could not confide in anyone, after his first glimpse of the love of his life on TV - on MY TV show. Except me. Not the other Beatles. Not Brian Epstein. Not (obviously) Cynthia. Not Peter Brown, Brian's discreet assistant, or Neil Aspinall or Derek Taylor or any of the others. Only me, because I had been there on Day One.

John set about getting to meet and seduce Yoko. He obtained invitations to art exhibitions and parties. And kept me informed about his progress. Yoko was not the predator. If anyone, John was. But it was clear to me that he knew it was total, 100% love, not just physical attraction. And so it turned out to be.

Both were married with children. It broke all the socially acceptable rules.

80
That's All Folks!

But it was written.

John was very tactile - always hugging me, holding onto my arm. But one time in 1965 he and I were in a club - I think it was The Cromwellian - and without the girls - there were a couple of very cute Scandinavians there at a table. Short blonde hair, boyish looking. John nudged me. "Let's go over and talk to them".

They had no idea who we were - this was in 1965 - but seemed to enjoy our company. "Let's all go back to your flat", said John. I felt a bit odd, because of my friendship with Cynthia, but what the hell… so we asked them; they agreed and we leapt into a taxi.

At St Andrews Mansions, praised on TV by (then) Prince Charles, where I was living at the time, I had several bedrooms. A marvellous old block from centuries gone by, without such new fangled modern things as an elevator, it had been my Mother's mother's flat; when she died, almost the very minute that I was born, my father had taken it over for executives to stay the night when visiting the Tootals office in Cavendish Square nearby.

So it consisted of three bedrooms with a double bed in one - mine - and twin beds in the other two. A small sitting room for music, a bathroom, kitchen, toilet and a long passageway between them all. A rather odd, dark place actually, but location, location and remember I was only 20.

Those two guest rooms became the place where many 1960s pop and film people stayed overnight - or even, as in Jimi Hendrix's case, for some days after arriving in the UK whilst they searched for a home. Jimi's manager was my friend, the Animals guitarist Chas Chandler. He begged me to put Jimi up, which I agreed to do. No problem; he was a delight - a quiet, shy gentleman - much more elsewhere.

The long, deep, narrow bath in which I nearly lost my life after Daisy Mae Williams fainted after her orgasm, see another volume, was just one part of the dated furnishings.

The flat is still there - up two flights of wrought iron stairs. I visited it last year - it was being totally renovated and I watched the workmen removing the old bath and toilet on which I had sat many times - 60 years later it was headed to the skip.

Back to the Sixties - I politely made four cups of tea and we retired to one of the bedrooms and stripped off. It quickly became clear that the girls were not in the slightest bit interested in us, and were only concerned with their friend.

So John and I rather perfunctionally satisfied each other, went next door to the music room and played records all night. That was our one and only sexual encounter. Pleasant, but not worth repeating and neither

80
That's All Folks!

of us ever mentioned it again.

Funnily enough a few weeks later Brian Epstein and I were having our regular Thursday lunch and he asked me if I fancied any of "the boys".

"Not really", I replied, "though Paul is quite cute".

"Oh, you won't stand a chance there, dear. Paul is one of those boys who is so straight it doesn't bother him at all if any guy fancies him. He's flattered but hasn't got the slightest flicker of interest in anything gay. You might think about trying something with John, though". I didn't tell him we already had.

Brian believed, and I think quite rightly, that he was the worst manager of all time. He felt completely out of his depth, knew nothing about the job he was doing and was constantly worried he'd be found out as a fraud.
I think I was the only person he ever discussed this with - like his sex life, about which I was totally informed, often replying "too much information Brian".

I've told elsewhere how in a club one night I'd taken off my shirt to dance sweatily on the floor, collapsing on the seat next to him and he looked at me and said "You know you've probably got the best body of anyone in the music scene"… pause… "pity about the face".

He then threw his hands over his mouth in horror and said "Oh, my God, I can't believe I just said that - I'm so sorry".

I roared with laughter - "Don't worry Brian; I'm delighted to know you don't fancy me".

I adored Brian and he loved me. He knew I wasn't after anything. At one point he'd offered to manage me and I'd smiled sweetly and declined. He didn't have many real friends. Everyone either worked for him or were rough trade. He liked to be dominated, even beaten. Hefty builders. Or soldiers suited him fine.

The weekend before he died, he begged me to go down to his house in the country with him.

"Why? I don't do drugs and you'll want to do drugs. We don't fancy each other. Why?".

"Because I'll be lonely".

I laughed. "Come on, dear. Find a male hooker". I'd moaned at him on behalf of friends "why do you always over pay the hustlers?" And he'd replied "Cause then they think I'm groovy".

The "boys" as he called them were away in India with some guru. He did indeed take too many drugs, got bored, came back to London, took more drugs and died. I was terribly upset. Lesson one, on being totally selfish.

We used to lunch in an Italian restaurant on King's Road or Fulham Road - same place, same table, same day of the week if we were both in town at the same time. Once I said to him "I'm sorry Brian but I'm going to stop having lunch with you, unless you stop taking drugs".

80
That's All Folks!

"What do you mean?".

"Well, I'll be in the middle of a fascinating anecdote and your eyes glaze over and look over my head, not hearing a word I'm saying".

"Oh, my dear, I'm sorry; it's not the drugs - it's every now and then a beautiful boy walks down the street behind you".

Remember, I'd first met him, thanks to the wonderful Derek Taylor - see elsewhere, before I became Jonathan so he always called me Ken and we had a different relationship. In fact my first hit had kept his group The Beatles off the No1 slot on the charts with Help! One week only but it gave me "satisfaction" - another of my hits, as Bubblerock. I charted under so many pseudonyms.

He was terribly insecure - being just that decade or so older than I was and very much in the generation where it was a crime, not just a sin, to be gay.

Also he was from Liverpool. I love that city and almost all Scousers - that magic mix of Irishness in them. But a very anti-gay place in the 1950s. Even though, by the 60s, being gay was still a crime, the UK was a far more relaxed society. The law was changed in 1967. But he'd never met someone like me who was so completely, totally relaxed about sexuality.

The Bowie/Bolan/Glitter years were yet to come. But

those of us freely mixing in London, the capital of the world in the 1960s, were genuinely absolutely tolerant in both worlds - sexuality and drug experimentation were not only allowed but approved of. "Do your own thing; do not obey ancient, out dated social rules".

The fact that I was also clearly and openly not into drugs - they were not for me - yet also not condemning anyone for feeling otherwise - made my open attitude to sexuality refreshing to many. I did not preach any position. Each to their own. I knew what my morality was and kept to it but didn't push it on anyone else.

I did tell Brian many times why I did not do drugs and we discussed it. He saw my point of view. And I used to tell him he'd never be able to live without drugs until he sorted out the other demons inside him. I only wish he'd found a soulmate. He deserved one - he was a lovely person. I warned him about rough trade - just as I warned many friends in pop about underage groupies. Ironic, considering future events.

I regret both Brian and John failing to be around today. I'm sure we would have remained close friends. I'd be visiting Brian every week in his care home - he'd be in his 90s now - pushing him around the garden in his wheelchair, taking frequent breaks to rest my tired bones on the odd memorial bench, discussing old times, chiding him for forgetting.

80
That's All Folks!

And John would probably still be in New York, very much my second city or home. Whenever I could I'd pop over to the Dakota building - two minutes walk away from me on 57th Street - and we'd go to Mets games or talk about Julian and Sean and Paul and I'd go on about George bashing in that fan's nose when she belittled him in Surrey and how he'd sweetly sneaked out of his hotel in Chicago to buy a single for me, solely because the singer, too, was a KING (Ramona) that he'd heard on the radio. George could always spot a good song - it was never a hit for Ramona but later went on to become huge for Betty Everett as The Shoop Shoop Song and then Cher as It's In His Kiss.

George actually made my favourite Beatle solo records, though we fell out when my version of He's So Fine was played in court, to illustrate the similarity to his My Sweet Lord - he never spoke to me again, after losing the case. My version remains amusing. Though clearly not to him.

My favourite John song ever was #9 Dream. My favourite Paul song - and there are not many, oddly, considering we both loved Buddy Holly - is Live And Let Die. There is no such thing as a favourite Ringo one.

I wrote and sang a song in the 70s called When I Was A Star - based on the Michel Delpech French original. I had a few hits with my English versions of French, Italian,

Spanish and Dutch songs - Michel also wrote Flirt. It was my idea of reaching my 80s and seeing all my old school/pop friends ("Who'd have thought in Rod's band/ That he'd be King of Scotland?"). It was a small hit. "I had lunch with Elton - with his long white hair". It's an amusing lyric actually, seen from the viewpoint of me at 84. John and Yoko are included.

But it also throws a light on the different worlds of then, now and the future. One young friend of mine, in his late twenties, asked me "Who is Rod Stewart?". I wonder whether, in twenty years time, the name Elton John will mean anything. Fame is fleeting. Leaders and tyrants like Churchill, Hitler, JFK, Stalin, Netanyahu, Trump and Putin will mean less than Attila the Hun in a century or so.

Yet we cherish "celebrities" so much when they mean so little. Look at this volume of memoires - many will buy it and read it because of "stars", like those mentioned herein and elsewhere. But blink, in the fullness of time when this is read in 2125, and only historians with dandruff on collars, pince nez perched on noses and musty, dusty voices will know or care who Jonathan King was. Their lectures on me in University Halls of future history will simply inspire disinterest or sleep in the students thronging the benches.

And fame changes just as the music does. Famous

80
That's All Folks!

people in 2025 include Taylor Swift and BTS yet almost nobody, today, at the height of their fame, could name a hit or hum a tune of theirs. Except for their tiny army of fans and those attracted by their physical appeal, they are non stars. Walk past any of them in the street and you'd not recognise them.

"Oh I know him", you'd think about the other JK, Jung Kook, "he was the waiter in the Korean restaurant I went to last night". Or "I know her - isn't she the daughter of that girl who was in Titanic with Leo DeCaprio in the 1990s?".

And name a recent Number One chart hit. Go on, name it.

Chart value destroyed, unintentionally, sadly, by me. Ruining the era of mass appeal smashes when everyone, young or old, middle aged or lovers of jazz or classics, knew Who Let The Dogs Out or I Get Knocked Down But I Get Up Again (my last two real hits) whether they hated, loved or felt indifferent about them.

"You can talk", you will say. Quite right too. Most of those who might remember my old hits, and I sang on 40 million records sold, under different names, are either dead of old age or deaf and suffering senility. Time moves on, very few are remembered. I'm still here.
Just.

Chapter 9

MONEY

I've made a lot of money over the 80 years of my life. Many millions. And many, many more millions for others. Most of all the British treasury. In the 1960s under a Labour government and Prime Minister Harold Wilson, income tax was 95 pence in the pound. You kept 5 pence for every pound you earned. Ridiculous.

Only just out of my teens in 1965, this was a hefty chunk to pay. My brilliant partners and producers, Joe Roncoroni and Ken Jones, advised me to get a crack accountant and to set up a company - that paid far less tax. I think about 20% as opposed to 95%.

So I had a meeting with Aubrey Byrne, accountant to the stars, and set up Jonathan King Enterprises Limited, which exists to this day.

Remember, as a singer I was earning a tiny royalty at the time - 2 or 3% - standard for the era, as producers paid the massive studio and musician costs and took the risk which, 99 times out of a hundred, ended in them

80
That's All Folks!

losing everything. Also, as I've said, Ken's brilliant arrangement and production of Everyone's Gone To The Moon, slowing it down, putting it in waltz tempo, adding soaring strings and making me sing it in two, plaintive ways, one dry, one with echo, was responsible for it becoming the global hit it did, with 9 million copies sold.

And I had written it. That was far more rewarding financially - meaning I was paid every time it was on the radio and every time someone else sang it, from Frank Sinatra to Marlene Dietrich, Doris Day, Nina Simone and others - including dozens of instrumentals by the likes of Percy Faith, Mantovani and conductors of orchestras. Liberace even recorded it.

Which brought me in peanuts, in today's money, but millions back then, enabling me to do what I really wanted to do - produce. Ranging from my second, self penned Top Five hit It's Good News Week for Hedgehoppers Anonymous and then groups and acts like Genesis, The Bay City Rollers and other musicians linked to my label or publishers like 10cc, Abba, The Rocky Horror Show and the rest.

But I was still not in the slightest bit interested in money. It attached itself to me - often despite me. When, getting bored with Genesis, I persuaded Tony Stratton Smith to take them over for me, he was a penniless Daily Sketch football journalist who happened to be using a spare office on the ground floor of MY office in 37 Soho Square. I almost had to force Tony. I'd produced his little band The Koobas for him in 1966 with a couple of songs. I told him that it wasn't that he was a great manager but a) his office was in my building, b) I liked him and thought him honest, decent and straight - financially, c) I could guarantee him the kids would be enormous because they were talented or, at least, the singer Peter had a superb voice and d) because I had started them, named them and was now bored by it.

They would make millions but I didn't want a penny from them, as I'd failed to break them. I even refused to take a small royalty for having given them their name. "If I'd broken them, yes", I said, "since I failed, it would be morally wrong".

Tony called me a couple of years later. "I hate you", he said.

"Oh, why?".

"Because Genesis are really beginning to break on my label, Charisma, and I decided, because I promised you, that it wasn't right for me to negotiate their new deal with myself, if I was their manager, so I took on a brilliant young kid, Tony Smith, to manage them who has screwed the most enormously huge amount out of me - all because I promised you to be honest".

"Don't worry, dear", I said, "you will be rewarded in

80
That's All Folks!

heaven. Let's have lunch. I'll pay".

Tony was also gay and we had wonderful gossip sessions together. He died far too young. A lovely guy. He gave up writing about football thanks to Genesis. Or, rather, thanks to me. The Koobas never happened though - I seem to remember their drummer Tony ended up drumming with YES.

I've told how my dear friend and mentor Sir Edward Lewis, who had founded and owned the mighty Decca record company, with EMI the biggest music labels in the world, told his wife, just before he died, that I was the only person he had ever met in his life who hadn't wanted anything from him. She asked him "what about me?". He replied "you want and get love. And give it in return. But he simply cares about music; finding, making, breaking good music. And doesn't want anything for it".

He was right. The satisfaction was enough. But I did find that I'd look behind me and there was money pouring into my bank account without my caring or noticing.

I go into far greater detail about Sir Edward, Decca and the many talented, and no longer talented, people involved elsewhere. When he asked me to look after the company he said "there are a lot of people here who should have retired years ago" he was in his late 60s himself "but they were really helpful in the past - please don't fire them or even let them feel unused". I explain in Volume One how I achieved that.

In the late 60s, when I was virtually running Decca as a favour to Sir Edward, paid nothing except expenses which were, admittedly, enormous - first class flights; always 5 star hotels, my mother, who was also my book keeper and, with Aubrey Byrne, in charge of my finances, called me up and said "you're about to run out of money".

Rather unusually, she thought, I gave up my unpaid job and decided to make some more hit records. Astonishingly, that was what happened. Hit after hit, top producer of the year several times, 40 million records sold as a singer under a variety of names from Shag to The Weathermen, Piglets to Nemo, The Sun Had Got His Hat On - although I was only making music because I loved it.

Which caused me to form U K Records, the most successful little label ever, though owing a lot to Brit Records, the forerunner to Island, as often discussed with Chris Blackwell, and inspired by several American startups, most failures but all showing the way to do it.

But none of my projects, from Genesis through Abba, 10cc, The Bay City Rollers, The Rocky Horror Show, made me as much money as they should have done, if I had been interested in making money.

80
That's All Folks!

Which I never was, never have been and, to this day, do not care about.

Oh, I've been sensible. My lifestyle these days is essentially luxury. But it's done on a shoe string budget, funded from my pension. I stay in the cheapest rate deal five star hotels with vast costs deducted through the Frequent Flyer deals. The best, for me, is ACCOR, ALL, which just saved me £1000 on a month's stay in the South of France.

At home I own my house, bought for £18,650 in 1967, so no rent. I cook most of my own meals and for many friends, who love my cuisine. Hotels all know me well, are delighted to have a guest whose Rolls Royce parked in front enhances the reputation of their establishment and which upgrades me automatically from my booked and paid for tiny box room to the Presidential Suite every visit.

Top restaurants deduct 50% as a matter of principle for a regular, elderly, handsome client so I pay, for a five star gourmet meal, the equivalent to a McDonalds family outing. Oh, that's the other thing, I'm on my own. No ghastly expensive wives or dreadful spoilt children, demanding caviar with ketchup on their burgers.

When he was dying from leukaemia, Sir Edward offered to give me Decca. At the time worth 85 million quid, a lot of money back then. As long as I promised to run it for the rest of my life, never to sell it.

I declined. Telling him I hated running companies, had only done it for him (twice) as a favour, was delighted to have dropped U K Records and never wanted to run a company ever again, but I loved him dearly and asked him please not to die.

Je ne regrette rien.

In 2000 Eric Nicoli, then boss of EMI, the other great British record company, offered me £5 million a year on a firm 10 year contract to be global Chairman of EMI. I accepted. Because I felt, by then, at 56, I knew enough to be able to run the company at arms length, with trusted Lieutenants to take care of stock holders, human resources, taxes and so on whilst I simply found, made, developed, broke and promoted great music.

It would be, today the biggest music company in the world. My concept for it in 2000 included basic online ideas for the sites that essentially became both iTunes and YouTube. It would have funded the Treasury. It would have stopped the decline of music into a second rate service industry.

But it was not to be. Max Clifford, on behalf of Brits in America about to lose their jobs - so I believe, and with the help of Surrey Police and the broken judicial system - stopped my career in music dead in the winter of the year 2000. Max lived to regret it. Just.

80
That's All Folks!

I explained to Eric in 1999 that the advent of online music services like Napster would mean increasing amounts of online business. Though I predicted never more than 5-10%, that was still a hefty, multi million chunk of income. So I would form an online department of EMI that would look after all internet rights to our music and also represent the music of the other big labels, none of whom knew or cared about online.

We would start online music radio and TV services - featuring the best music, not just our own product. We would control sales online - then called "downloads". We would link up with retailers so anybody going into a shop for advice could download tracks, through them, at a cheaper rate than doing it direct themselves at home, with a small sum going to the shop.

So a Springsteen fan, for example, buying a new vinyl album by The Boss in the shop, might be played some Tom Petty tracks and might end up downloading them, through the retail site, at a slightly cheaper rate than if they did it direct themselves. Plus they would have been made aware of the tracks by helpful music lovers, working in the shops. Or they might have heard them on our radio shows or seen them on our video shows. And coming with the downloads, purchased at cut rate through retailers, would be free posters, booklets, photos and other gifts.

Radical, but good ideas for the new century, 2000. Not costing a lot - a small additional division for EMI globally, using all the existing departments for admin, contracts, royalties etc... that were already part of the corporation.

It would have worked for EMI. After all it did years later for iTunes, You Tube, Spotify and others. Remember - even MY SPACE didn't exist in 1999.

I just came across my detailed plan for EMI, buried away in a drawer. Using the huge asset of people who cared about music and worked in the record shops. Using the very best promotion people in the USA, many of whom were personal friends - one used to get me seats to the Super Bowl and to the World Series at cut prices.

The only serious music concept back then was a dodgy company called Napster. The concept was great but of no interest at all to the bosses of the music corporations, who had only just converted from vinyl, via cassette tapes to CDs.

These was just some of the many ideas I had to galvanise the British music corporation EMI into the largest global music company. It was not to be.

Que sera sera as one of my idols sang in the early 1960s in one of my favourite films The Man Who Knew Too Much. Doris Day, who went on to record her own special version of one of my songs.

80
That's All Folks!

I remain friends with the two executives I would have taken on to manage all those boring areas - Rupert Perry and Paul Conroy.

Since I was removed from the music industry, executives have concentrated on appealing to specialist fan areas. Profitable enough but with little or no mass appeal. Which was what made music in the 1960s and 1970s an essential, like food, drink and air. Sadly today it is a luxury extra.

Tastes have adapted too, as "hits" have changed. But as I write this the huge viral on TikTok is Una Paloma Blanca. And the biggest success sound from the modern Superhero movies was my OOGA CHAGGA version of Hooked On A Feeling from 1971. So perhaps tastes have not changed as much as the charts would make you think.

JONATHAN KING

Chapter 10

ROGUE DJS - KENNY EVERETT AND CHRIS DENNING

I've had so many messages, since my first volumes of this autobiography, asking about Kenny Everett, one of my dearest friends in the 1960s and a brilliant, original disc jockey.

I've detailed how the wonderful, floating pirate radio station Big L - or Radio London - along with Radio Caroline (North and South) played a huge part in my teenage life, not just as a fan but as a student and as an emerging pop star. These days, in this rather odd century, memories of the early days of radio and TV have faded and died but the UK, despite starting much of it, lagged far behind when it came to making the most of the media. Radio in particular was primitive in the early 1960s; predominantly Auntie BBC until the pirates came along, bringing American enthusiasm, a brand new British version of it and lots of music to our ears.

We teenagers had to depend on Radio Luxembourg

80
That's All Folks!

before that, which did play music to us, buried under our bedclothes. I still have my tiny transistor radio from way back then at pride of place on my mantelpiece at home. I could not have existed in the early 1960s without it. I look at it sometimes, and stroke it fondly.

Then the pirates began in 1964 and opened up a whole new world of excitement. Great DJs. Fabulous music. Mainly American but British because, after Bill Haley and the Comets and Elvis Presley came the explosion of extraordinary sounds from The Beatles.

I first heard them on the dear old BBC with Love Me Do, which I didn't like much but which, somehow, had an ingredient of magic. Then Please Please Me which was utterly different and destined to change everything about humanity. From Me To You. I truly believe that. I was there. I was part of it. I saw it affect morals, attitudes, politics, sexuality, recreational indulgence, growing up, becoming parents - the lot. But the hidden creativity, humour, originality of music was echoed in films and books with ingredients like James Bond, fashion - Carnaby Street, Mary Quant - and media.

Two enormous massive media moments in the 1960s were Top of the Pops on BBC TV and pirate radio. I cannot explain how huge the effect of these two things was on my generation of Brits and, rapidly, on the entire world - indeed more than the world. My Everyone's

JONATHAN KING

Gone To The Moon was one of the first pop tracks to be taken to the moon a couple of years later - the choice of astronaut Michael Collins on Apollo 11.

In fact, as explained elsewhere, the success of my first hit was down to Tony "Wendy" Windsor, the head Radio London DJ who played it three times in a row saying "I love this record; let's hear it again". The next day it sold 30,000 copies. When Wendy came off the boat I threw my arms around him and thanked him. "Oh, it was only because I couldn't get the other turntable to work", he said. I became a star by accident, due to a mechanical malfunction. Appropriate.

I was firm friends with several of the DJs on all the pirates and visited the ships a few times - there are photos in Volume One. Maurice Coles - the real name of Kenny Everett - was a young Scouse lad the same age as me born on Christmas Day 1944. He was incredibly inventive and full of ideas. There are many different types of Disc Jockey. Most just play records and introduce them. Others are devoted to talking, which I did in New York in the 1980s and later on Talk Radio in the UK. There were characters like Jimmy Savile, who used the position to establish a brand of celebrity. Some invented worlds, using the music as part of the structure and Kenny was one of the first of those, essentially building works of art.

He did shows on Big L with another DJ, Canadian

80
That's All Folks!

Dave Cash. Both became friends and used to stay in my flat when they came off the ships - the schedule was two weeks on; one week off in 1965 and 1966.

Kenny was gay and a virgin. He was a sweet little elfin faced boy with a great sense of humour, pale skin, bright eyes. Totally naive and innocent, fascinated by my tales of teenage debauchery. Incredibly shy - he never even dared to admit to anyone else that he was gay.

At a party one night in Brian Epstein's house in Chapel Street he fell in love with Brian's assistant, who was a good friend of mine. Kenny didn't even speak to him but confided to me afterwards that Peter was "the most gorgeous man I've ever seen". I called Peter who said he thought Kenny was very cute. And so Cuddly Ken lost his virginity.

Over the years we spent a lot of time together. I basically gave him future hits. Harry Nilsson was one - first played to me as demos by Davy Jones of The Monkees in Los Angeles. I introduced him to the Beatles set. He taught me many radio tricks, like talking to himself, as another character, on tape. He was brilliant at editing. We bounced off each other in humour - I'd have an idea; he'd develop it; I'd take over; then he'd refine it.

Kenny's problem was that he'd been let down so many times in life that he constantly pushed the boundaries of all relationships until eventually everyone - from business to friends - said "I've had enough" and walked away, thus proving him right, in his own mind, that they had never really loved him and had only pretended - quite rightly as he was, in his heart, a shit. He wasn't, but I know so many people like him.

This was the reason he was so often fired from key radio and TV jobs and he lost friends and lovers like there was no tomorrow which, for him, there rarely was. We never fell out, though we drifted apart. I introduced him to his wife Lee - on a visit down to my Mum's house, in Surrey, we had dropped by at Billy Fury's nearby home. Billy's girlfriend at the time was fellow Scouser Lee Middleton. She and Ken clicked immediately. Years later, at their wedding, I kept muttering "this is all a terrible mistake" which it was, though they remained dear friends to each other forever.

When, in later life, Kenny was diagnosed with Aids, in the early days when there was no cure, we had a long and lovely lunch which went on for hours, catching up, reminiscing, happy memories. As we kissed and hugged and said Goodbye he said "I'd forgotten how much I love Sagittarians". Typical! He died a couple of weeks later. One of my favourite people.

I remember once, after he and Lee split up, I visited her, in her flat, for tea. She was baking - she was a great baker - providing hot cakes for me and her other guest

80
That's All Folks!

Dusty Springfield, who I called Rusty Springboard, of course. In my opinion one of the greatest female singers of all time, along with Aretha Franklin and Gladys Knight.

Dusty was so relaxed knowing she could trust both of us and told me the only man she had ever fancied - "the only feller I ever wanted to f*** me" she said, delicately - was Scott Walker and that she was terribly jealous of me. I told her that, to both my and Scott's eternal sadness, we never actually had sex. It had been a genuine total bromance. She was rather disappointed.

When Dusty was dying, years later, I called her up and said I wished we'd been closer friends. She said the same about me.

Another DJ on Radio London was Chris Denning. He had been on Radio Luxembourg, like Johnny Moran, my first friend in the DJ world. Both were eventually recruited by the BBC to launch Radio One, when the pirates were made illegal.

That in itself was quite an adventure. A very junior BBC producer, Johnny Beerling, was sent out, undercover, with me, to the ships - I was the official visitor; he was, and remains, my friend. It was all very secret - the BBC could not be seen to encourage any contact with pirates.

Eventually Angela Bond was given Kenny to produce

and control at the Beeb - an impossible task in both cases. She was a lovely, beaky, bespectacled lady who became close to all of us. Johnny later became the best and most successful Controller of Radio One.

Chris Denning had a very good radio voice and presence. He had been consensually raped as a child by an American soldier, if my recollection is correct, in Germany but it was not considered rape at the time, either by him, the "gorgeous" American nor society. Either because of this, or through genetics, Chris was gay too - and fancied teenage boys but, probably because of those first pre-puberty, he assured me, encounters was only interested in mutual masturbation. In fact he said he'd been a "rent boy" in his teens, only providing that basic service. Anything involving penetration of any orifice offended him.

Chris went prematurely bald - he said his American had a close, blond crew cut and thought he might have psychologically inherited the hair situation. He wore the most appalling toupee. But had a great sense of humour. He, Kenny and I laughed all the way through the late 60s, after the pirates were outlawed - the two of them hosted a show on the BBC called Where It's At - a terrible catch phrase of the time.

The first time I ran Decca for Sir Edward I persuaded Chris to take over promotion, under me, based in the

80
That's All Folks!

Great Marlborough Street offices. He was a terrific salesman and gave up DJing to devote himself to plugging the records to radio and TV, with spectacular results. We had numerous hits. One day I was summoned to Sir Edward's office and was told that Chris had been "let go", with a substantial payment.

"Why?" I asked. No reason was given. Neither was it to Chris, when I quizzed him, and he didn't care, as he'd been offered a similar but much better paid job at Bell Records. I assumed that had been the reason he'd left Decca.

I shrugged my shoulders and took on Don Wardell, another DJ from Radio Luxembourg, to be Head of Promotion. It was around then that I discovered I had no money left, and stopped the Decca job to concentrate on producing, writing and singing. We're talking 1970 here.

So successful was my production career that I was persuaded by my American lawyer Paul Marshall to start my own label; UK Records - and I immediately hired Denning to run the UK side of the company and Wardell to look after America, based in New York.

Before I hired Chris I made him promise, on his mother's life, never to do anything that might reflect badly on the label. I was aware of his tastes and the dangers potentially - remember, the legal age of consent between males at that time was 21. He swore he would stick to the rules.

But he didn't, and friends later told me I should have known. It was not in his nature - as he said to me "I couldn't help myself". Looking back, and it took me years, it's now obvious what caused the breach with Decca - clearly an angry parent had contacted the company. But I had truly believed him. When I found out that he was being investigated by police and he shamefully admitted the truth to me, I let him leave and never saw him again.

Actually he had not been any good at running the company - great at promotion; not great at administration. We kept in touch with letters and through mutual friends - not, as inaccurately reported in Wikipedia and other media sources, after he was convicted - but his life slowly became more and more spent in prison cells all over the world. Cost me a fortune in stamps. He read and loved 65 My Life So Far and sent me loads of corrections and notes from it.

A few years ago I was contacted by a stranger who claimed to have been inside with Denning in England, who said Chris had always spoken fondly of me, and that he had been transferred to another jail, in which he had just died, under mysterious circumstances, with no media coverage at all.

I investigated - contacting the Home Office and the

80
That's All Folks!

Governor of the prison concerned. Nothing. No denial. No confirmation. Nothing. Except refusal to assist.

Years later it was revealed that he had, indeed, become ill, requiring emergency treatment in hospital that had not been provided by the prison, which was strongly condemned by a "government report" - just another example of too late, too little, too old to concern anybody. He was, by then, in his 80s. A broken system. Unable to do the job. I remember when the ghastly David Blunkett was Home Secretary and it was reported that Dr Harold Shipman had died in prison, Blunkett said he "cracked open a bottle". The man responsible for the care of prisoners - no matter what their crimes - celebrated a death in custody. His custody. Shocking.

It was like the IPP situation - keeping someone in jail forever "for public protection"; a wicked, evil, wrong policy which was swiftly condemned and made illegal but thousands still remained in prison, serving well beyond their sentence. As I write, the furore over this has caused a report to be made which condemns it and says those inmates should be released within weeks. We shall see. Exposure of the prison system is well overdue.

Chris was a fantastic promotion man and a decent DJ. He was also gay and found teenage boys attractive. For that, in the last and present century, he was jailed and has now been killed. Nobody cares. That is the true tragedy.

Both Kenny and Chris led unwise lives. Who hasn't? Both paid the price - for Kenny, for promiscuity in an era before cures were discovered; for Chris, I suspect, for trusting unsuitable partners and police prepared to assist age re-invention. And both, because morality changes over the decades. And media changes with it. A better story.

I like to remember the many good sides of each character, and the many others I've met over the past 80 years. And shall continue to do so. Who knows what the world will make of me, after I've croaked. I shall be beyond caring. But will you?

80
That's All Folks!

In the summer of 2025, JK poses for a selfie

Peter Frampton in his HERD days 1960s

Bowie with two Framptons, and Peter today

Sir Edward Lewis with Roy Orbison

Ronnie Campbell MP, JK and Jonathan Aitken in the House of Commons 2005

J K on right with glasses; Nigel middle front row

The Early Radio London Fab Forties
Sunday 15th August 1965

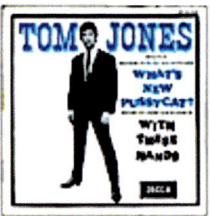

As this pic sleeve shows, on the continent 'What's New Pussycat' and 'With These Hands' was a do[uble] first (Decca F12191) c/w 'Untrue', while 'Pussycat' (Decca F12203) had a song called 'Rose' as its B[-side, in] order, 'Hands' reaching #13, 'Pussycat' climbing to #11. However, the reverse is happening in this w[eek's chart] while 'Hands' slides from #15 to #33!

'What's New Pussycat' is the title track from Woody Allen's first major film, which also starred Pet[er Sellers,] by Burt Bacharach is here.)

Last Week	This Week		
4	1	Everyone's Gone To The Moon	Jonathan King
3	2	Help!	Beatles
6	3	I Want Candy	Brian Poole & the Tremeloes
2	4	Catch Us If You Can	Dave Clark Five
1	5	We've Gotta Get Out Of This Place	Animals
10	6	Zorba's Dance	Marcello Minerbi
24	7	I Got You Babe	Sonny & Cher

Ozzy Osbourne and his wife Sharon - two of the nicest people in music I ever met. Here I'm dressed as The Pope before introducing Ozzy to the crowd at Donington 1986.

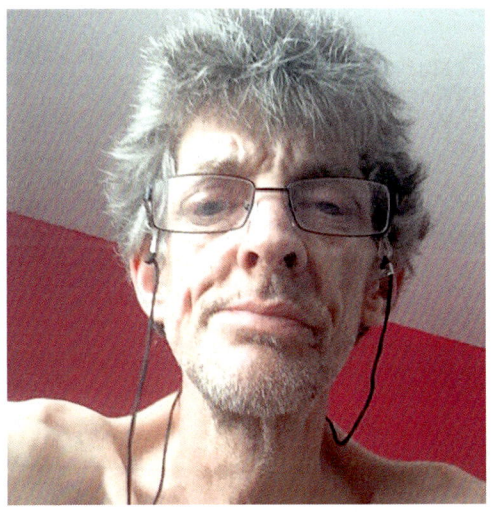

Christopher Sealey 2010

Katrina Leskanich 1997

DISASTER!

EVEN THOUGH THE VIEWING FIGURES FOR SHOW 2 SERIES 4 OF "ENTERTAINMENT U.S.A." WENT UP TO

5.79 MILLION (M.R.I.B.)

LAST WEEK, WE SLIPPED FROM No. 1 TO THE No. 3 SHOW ON THE BBC 2 TOP TEN CHART.

THIS IS NOT GOOD ENOUGH!!!

THE BEST T.V. PROGRAMME ON THE AIR MUST ALSO BE THE MOST WATCHED
AT LEAST ON OUR CLASSY CHANNEL!

PLEASE HELP. SPREAD THE WORD. DISCUSS IT WITH YOUR FRIENDS AND FAMILY. FORM CONCERNED CITIZEN GROUPS. THIS WEEK OUR OPPOSITION WAS "THE MISS WORLD CONTEST" AND RUMOUR HAS IT THAT SEVERAL VIEWERS MAY HAVE TUNED TO ITV FOR SOME INCOMPREHENSIBLE REASON. HELP MAKE GREAT TELEVISION DOMINATE THE NATIONS SETS.

THURSDAYS. 9.00p.m. B.B.C.2.

THE MOST VIDEOTAPED SHOW ON BRITISH T.V.

The married father was also forced to resign from his post on the Victims and Survivors Panel of the Independent Inquiry into Childhood Sexual Abuse, the public investigation into systemic sexual abuse in schools, churches and other institutions.

Peter Saunders, 61, founded the National Association for People Abused in Childhood. He was arrested after having a sexual encounter in a restaurant toilet with a woman he knew had been molested as a youngster

An IICSA spokesman said he had failed to declare the incident when he joined in 2015, adding: 'The inquiry holds our consultative panel members to the same high standards we expect of our staff. Peter Saunders offered his resignation and we have accepted it with immediate effect.'

Kenny Everett and Dave Cash taking broadcasting seriously

Re: SEALEY contacting member of PRESS re sale of story.

31/15D

STATEMENT NUMBER: S 101

Receiver's Instructions : Action YES / NO   Sign/Date CL2007 15/2

Receiver to complete ACTION REQUIRED	Indexer to Action No	complete Sign/Date	
TRS		CL2007	15/2
		CL2007	1/10/01

The original statement taken with O'Brien regarding Sealey taken 15th February 2001 - note the date for Typing and Filing (01/10/01 - October 1st 2001) and signature C Loving PC2007

Form MG 11 (CONT)

Page No. ...Four...

Continuation of Statement of: S M O'Brien.

to 6'0" tall. Naturally I bought him a drink and we began to discuss his story. He told me that he had met Jonathan KING when he was about 13 years old. He was on a visit to London with a friend. He said that it was either a record shop or an amusement arcade that they were located in when they were approached by KING. Although I believe that I was told he did not visit KING's home on that first meeting, he did subsequently go to KING's home on later visits, which he believed was in Kensington. He told me that over a

---

I was 14 years old at this time and I was fairly small and skinny for my age. I had medium length brown hair. I was carrying a Hamleys carrier bag which contained some cricket pads I had bought. I had used some money that I shouldn't have done to buy them and I remember telling my mum later that Jonathan KING had bought them for me. Whilst stood at the market stall KING carried on talking to me and he asked me if I had been in any of the peep shows. I told him that I had not and he then proceeded to tell me that there was a good one on the corner. He asked me if I wanted to go to one and I remember saying to him that I would not get in. I also told him that I had tried to get in a few but I had been told I was too young.

Signature: C A Sealey   Signature witnessed by:
2017

The two contradictory stories by SEALEY - the first that he had been with a friend and met me briefly in a record store; the second his Police and Court statement several years later. Understandable why Surrey Police would fail to disclose the first interview transcript to the defence or the court.

Heroin charges

A ST NEOTS man appeared in court on Thursday to face two counts of possessing heroin.

Christopher Sealey (29), of Spar House, was also charged with interfering with a vehicle and obstructing a police constable during a drugs search.

Sealey pleaded not guilty to one charge of possessing heroin and interfering with a vehicle.

He admitted another charge of possessing heroin and obstructing a police constable during a drugs search.

The case against Sealey was adjourned until April 6 for a pre-trial review to take place and he was released on unconditional bail.

FOX ASSOCIATES PRIVATE INVESTIGATORS 3, OSWIN ROAD LEICESTER LE3 1HR

0116-2751381

07850-355022 www.foxassociatespi.com
office@foxassociatespi.com 1st March 2017

Reference C. A SEALEY

On Friday the 17th of February 2017 at 8.19am I visited the home address (1, Pulleyn Court, St. Neots, Cambridgeshire. PE19 1RQ) of Christopher Alexander SEALEY born 04/03/1969.

I had roused Sealy from his sleep via intercom, had introduced myself as an investigator and gave him a basic reason for calling, which was his involvement in the Jonathan KING case.

I was buzzed in and then let into his ground floor flat, went with him into the living room. Initially, Sealey, was a little agitated, scratching and rubbing his face, but after a few minutes he became more lucid, apologised and explained to me that he had taken two sleeping tablets the night before.

Again - a previous crime not disclosed by police or CPS and not discovered by the lazy, incompetent defence team. And excerpts from DEAN SWANN's reports, when he investigated Sealey a decade ago.

He allowed me to take his photograph and was more than willing for me to have his mobile phone number, joking "as long as you don't bug it" (which subconsciously illustrated his suspicions about me). I have left him on good terms, he has my details and I told him he can call me at any time if he wishes to discuss this matter any further. I left at 0843hrs.

I had the feeling that Sealey, like many long-term drug addicts, has serious problems with the truth and could prepared to say almost anything a questioner would like him to say. He makes an extremely unreliable witness and I suspect he has difficulties sorting the truth from the lies, even in his own head.

Dean Swann

Dean Swann Fox Associates

An old friend

The love of my life - a 14th birthday present

SIX CHIX

I've always been intrigued by the differences in generations. I took this photo in Valbonne in 2025

Page 4 Opinion

Bowie's record does not deserve to die

Jonathan King's Column

TAKE ARMS! Defend the battlements! In the middle of the present stagnant pool of garbage, which pop music seems to have become, there is an island of hope that looks ready to be drowned undiscovered.

DAVID BOWIE has given us a record called "I can't Help Thinking About Me" and, although the backing is a little monotonous, the sound is good, the tune is catchy, the performance impeccable and the lyrics outstanding.

This is a disc which does not deserve to die because there are too few really enjoyable ones alive at the moment. I therefore suggest that every reader who has not heard it to do so.

If you disagree, let me know, but I can guarantee that a lot of you will be glad I brought it to your notice. Keep your ears open for the words in particular.

I was down at the Scotch watching STEVIE WONDER last week. Very good, very professional, and well worth seeing. But the scene down there brought a few things to mind which I feel might benefit us all by finishing.

Frequently now the clubs see "impromptu" sessions where famed and well-regarded artistes are dragged to the stage and told to perform free of charge. Last week saw Stevie Wonder joined by Georgie Fame, Keith Moon and Chris Farlowe.

The result — embarrassing and it nearly always is. Why? These musicians (and I don't cite the above in particular) all come from different fields. They all want to demonstrate how well they can play.

So we see six or seven soloists (often the most incompatible people imaginable) performing in six or seven ways. This is when I leap for the cotton wool.

The other thought that occurred to me was how dreary and dull today's so-called "soul" singers are becoming. The "I am singing right from my heart" brigade sounds like OTIS REDDING filtered through WILSON PICKETT and they are eternally rendering "They call me Mr. Pitiful in the midnight hour" in pseudo-Negro voices.

When I say "pseudo-Negro" I don't mean that most offenders are white. The majority are coloured and try their best to sound it.

I'm very glad to see ANDY OLDHAM has another Immediate hit on his hands with CHRIS FARLOWE'S "Think". It's a very interesting sound and I think that — although it could be the last hit on these lines — it incorporates some new ideas.

My last word of forboding is given to THE ANIMALS. They are all friends of mine, good people and talented performers, but MICKIE MOST is such a brilliant selector of songs that anyone lucky enough to be connected with him should stay that way.

I don't know where their first Decca record will finish up in the charts, but if it is not as high as expected it won't be because of the standard of their singing, playing or of Tom Wilson's production. It will be because the song is not commercial enough. Then it will be time for the Animals to ask Mickie to return to the fold.

My column in Music Echo

My girlfriend in the 1970s Janet Atkinson.

My girlfriend in the 1980s Samantha Fox.

Count 11

STATEMENT OF OFFENCE

INDECENT ASSAULT ON A MALE PERSON, contrary to Section 15(1) of the Sexual Offences Act 1956

PARTICULARS OF OFFENCE

Kenneth George King, on a day between the 1st day of March 1983 and the 2nd day of March 1984, indecently assaulted [redacted] a male person aged 15 years.

Count ~~17~~ 16

STATEMENT OF OFFENCE

INDECENT ASSAULT ON A MALE PERSON, contrary to Section 15(1) of the Sexual Offences Act 1956

PARTICULARS OF OFFENCE

Kenneth George King, on a day between the 26TH day of ~~August 1984~~ July 1985 and the 29 day of ~~September 1984~~, indecently assaulted [redacted] a male person aged ~~13~~ 14 years.

Count ~~18~~ 17

STATEMENT OF OFFENCE

ATTEMPTED BUGGERY, contrary to Section 1(1) of the Criminal Attempts Act 1981.

PARTICULARS OF OFFENCE

Kenneth George King, being a man over the age of 21 years, on a day between the 16TH day of ~~October 1984~~ and the 8th day of ~~February 1985~~, attempted to commit buggery with [redacted] a male person under the age of 21, being 13 years.

Count ~~21~~ 19

STATEMENT OF OFFENCE

INDECENT ASSAULT ON A MALE PERSON, contrary to Section 15(1) of the Sexual Offences Act 1956

PARTICULARS OF OFFENCE

Kenneth George King, on a day between the 3RD day of ~~January 1987~~ May 1989 and the ~~31st~~ 4TH day of ~~December 1987~~, indecently assaulted [redacted] a male person aged ~~12 or~~ years.

Can you believe this corrected (by hand) indictment after several date changes? This was exactly what was put to the jury including a mistake - the "13 year old" would have been 15 on the changed dates.

This was Deniz Corday aged 86 in 2015 before Surrey Police arrested him. Doctors told him he should have 10 more years of life.

This was Deniz in 2016, after the effects of Surrey Police questioning.
He died in January 2017.

Laurence Pollinger survived a motor bike crash when he was 20 but not after being falsely accused of being a victim by Surrey Police. "I very nearly died", he told me in 2015 and he did die, two days later, aged 56.

Rob Randall - The other person killed by Surrey Police in 2016 and not investigated by the IOPC, as it should have been. A very successful DJ in the 1960s and later.

One of my Editors Alex Day and his girlfriend Georgia. Thanks for the edits - and to my brother Andy, the other Editor.

JK in Paris

By KATIE FRENCH FOR MAILONLINE
PUBLISHED: 19:36, 20 June 2018 | UPDATED: 23:57, 20 June 2018

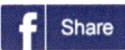

41 shares

A former DJ raped a teenager waiter after plying him with brandy, a court heard.

Jonathan King, 73, picked up the 14-year-old boy from outside luxury **London** hotel Claridge's where the young teen worked, a jury was told.

The victim was introduced to the pop personality through a friend in the 1970s but did not come forward until he heard of King's arrest for a separate charge in 2001.

The disgraced pop personality is accused of using his fame to lure youngsters for rides in his Rolls Royce where he would take them for dinner, drinks and tours of his luxury London flat.

The victim told jurors: 'I started working at Claridge's hotel at 14, part-time as a commis waiter. This was 1977 or 78.

He said the other waiter asked if he wanted to go out after work and said a friend was picking them up.

Mail Online

| Home | News | Royals | U.S. | Sport | TV | Showbiz | Femail | Health | Science | Money | T

Latest Headlines | Australia | Video | University Guide | Deep Dive | China | Debate | Meghan Markle | Princ

ADVERTISEMENT

Ex-DJ Jonathan King, 73, 'twice raped 14-year-old Claridge's waiter he picked up outside after plying him with brandy and boasting of threesomes with teenagers'

- Ex-DJ abused youngsters in 1970s and 1980s after giving them alcohol, jury told
- Victim spoke out when King bragged he was 'guilty of being good at seduction'
- King denies 17 charges of indecent assault on males aged between 16 and 21

By KATIE FRENCH FOR MAILONLINE
PUBLISHED: 19:36, 20 June 2018 | UPDATED: 23:57, 20 June 2018

So much wrong Media coverage - always inflated and often also factually inaccurate even compared to the prosecution claims.
All the evidence, produced by the defence, that this claim was a pack of lies, was never carried by any media.

DOCUMENT RECORD PRINT
Officer's Report
URN R41GL
TO: REF: STN/DEPT:
FROM: **HODGES, RICHARD** REF:
STN/DEPT: TEL/EXT:
SUBJECT: TITLE: Report re the release dates of Friday the Thirteenth and Meatballs.   DATE: 24/02/2017 12:07
N799 HODGES REPORTS ON FILM RELEASE DATES MENTIONED BY N502
In his ABE interview and subsequent statement (S138C), N502 X states that he was 14 or 14 and a half years of age when he started working at Claridges and when he met N595 RUTH. He states that he and RUTH became good friends and went to the cinema together where they saw the above two films. He says this happened within the first couple of months of knowing each other and **before the incidents with N3 KING.** X's date of birth is the 10/06/1964, so he would have been 14 on the 10/6/78 and 14 and a half on the 10/12/78, turning 15 on the 10/6/79.

RESEARCH INTO FILM, 'FRIDAY THE 13th'
This film is well documented on the internet and the IMDB website provides a specific UK release date for the film of the **05/08/1980**.
http://www.imdb.com/title/tt0080761/releaseinfo

MEATBALLS
Meatballs is not so well documented on the internet. There is a lot of information about the film itself which would seem to have been filmed in the early part of 1979 and was then released first in Canada on the 28/6/79. The imdb shows that the film was then released across the world in the coming months until 6/12/1981 when it was finally released in Ireland. There is however no listing for the UK release date.
http://www.imdb.com/title/tt0079540/releaseinfo?ref_=tt_ql_dt_2
I have completed extensive research online to try and date the release of this film in the UK and have enlisted the help of researcher CE SHAW however neither of us have been able to confirm a specific date, nor were we able to identify any fan clubs or groups who may provide reasonable lines of enquiry. We did however identify that Lionsgate Studios own the rights to the film.
I therefore spoke to a representative of Lionsgate Films UK who could find no specific information about the release date of the film but stated it was likely to be the same release date as in Ireland. She suggested I contact Lionsgate USA who may have knowledge. As a result on the 23/02/17 I spoke to a representative of Lionsgate USA who said that Lionsgate in it's current form did not commence trading until 1997 and the film was purchased from someone that knew who and had no records of that.
DC BRIDGE attended the British Library on the 22/2/17 and checked the archives for any mention of the film's release date but was able to find none.
From X I am aware that he saw the film at the ABC cinema that was on Edgware Road. This cinema closed in 1988 and the company ABC closed a short while later.
It is therefore not feasible to approach the cinema to establish release dates.
As a result of the above I approached the independent cinema office and a representative, Ellen REAY searched their databases for information but again could find no release date, she did however send the below information:
"I found an entry on the BBFC saying it was classified in September 1979. Films are often classified about a month before release date, so no accurate release date, but likely between October and December 1979."
REAY went on to say that the film would have been released later in Ireland as the censors were more demanding in those days in Ireland. I believe that all realistic and proportionate lines of enquiry have been completed with regards to establishing the release date of this film, we have not been able to ascertain a specific date.
45HQ020115J83-R41GL J83 HJ OP RAVINE 45HJ9468 WK1405,
Surrey.Police. Printed On: 26/09/2017 15:22:00 Page 1 of 2

DOCUMENT RECORD PRINT
CONCLUSIONS
On the 05/08/1980, the day that Friday The 13th was released, **X would have been 16 years and 2 months old**. X reports that he saw the films within weeks of each other, so it would appear that he was over sixteen at the time of these events. I note it is also unusual that if Meatballs was released in late 1979 that it would have remained at the cinema for up to ten months.
X has been approached by IO KAVANAGH to seek some clarity around this and X can only repeat that the events he describes are absolutely true and he has described them as he remembers them.
Report for information, IO 15820 HODGES.
45HQ020115J83-R41GL J83 HJ OP RAVINE
45HJ9468 WK1405.Surrey.Police.Printed On: 26/09/2017 15:22:00 Page 2 of 2

Astonishing that after senior Surrey Police had concluded the man had to have been OVER 16 (by his own admission) that the CPS still brought charges about "a 14 year old Claridges waiter". Luckily the Judge, seeing this evidence, refused to allow any retrials after the trial collapsed.

The Jeremy Bamber Campaign has expressed its anger that the CCRC approached the Essex force rather than go directly to Blake or Milbank. "Unbelievably, the CCRC just accepted this revisionist account, and endorsed the view that Ms Blake, and the New Yorker, had obtained this material under false pretences, and it was, consequently, not worth considering," it said.

The New Yorker has issued a statement saying: "Heidi Blake's piece was meticulously reported and scrupulously factchecked. The New Yorker stands by the story."

This is the third time the CCRC has reviewed Bamber's case. In 2002, his case was sent back to the appeal court on DNA evidence. A panel of three judges rejected the appeal. In 2011, the CCRC refused to refer the case, stating that the evidence did not raise a real possibility that the court would find his convictions unsafe.

The CCRC has been criticised for the percentage of submissions it refers back to the appeal court (currently about 2%); its failure to investigate cases; the time it takes to deal with submissions; its work from home policy; and for not having the legal minimum number of commissioners.

From The Guardian July 2025

Exhibit A

I flew to New York to prepare for filming the new series of Entertainment USA on 22nd August 1985 on Pan Am 101 Clipper Class (see following pages both passport and Pan Am Worldpass list).
I attended Bruce Springsteen's Giants Stadium concert on the weekend of 1st September with, I believe, Capital Radio DJ Roger Scott (see Sun column of Sept 5th and letter of Sept 6th).
I had lunch on Sept 6th with my American accountant Alan Brout (see credit card slip and note).
I took my friend Ursula Kenny to see Back To The Future on Sept 7th, as she would certainly have testified had I been allowed to call her (see letter).
I went to the US Open Tennis Men's Final on Sept 8th (see original hand written King In New York broadcast in July 1983 with the mention at the top of page two illustrating my interest in Ivan Lendl, who I'd interviewed on my US radio show in 1980/81) when Lendl beat McEnroe to win the title (see Sun column of Sept 12th; witness statement from Paul Marshall; Souvenir programme from US Open pages).
I flew back to London on Sept 9th on Pan Am 2 Clipper Class (see Pan Am Worldpass list).
I collected my new visa for filming in the USA on Sept 10th. (see letters and passport).
I flew back to New York to start filming Entertainment USA on Sept 12th Pan Am 101 Clipper Class (see list and passport).
I attended the MTV Awards at Radio City Music Hall on Sept 13th (see Sun column dated 19th Sept).
I started filming Entertainment USA on Sept 16th.

This is just one page of the appeal submitted to the CCRC after I discovered evidence that I was in America during the period of the final, changed dates on the indictment - an alibi I was not allowed to find at trial after the dates were changed for the third time.

Virginia Giuffre is still considered "a reliable witness" despite numerous examples of her total dishonesty. Even her own family rejected many of her lies, causing her to kill herself. Of course, now she's dead those inheriting her wealth declare she spoke the truth at all times. And most of the public still believe. It's easier.

Nino Mulas

My friend Scott

The visual definition of the word SMUG.

80
That's All Folks!

JONATHAN KING

Chapter 11

THE SECOND POLICE BITE AT MY CHERRY

I blame it all on Jimmy Savile. Not himself, the poor sod, who I have discussed in 70 FFFY. But the media hype behind him, partly inspired by the vile Mark Williams Thomas, the ex Surrey cop turned muck raking journalist, via a stint as a "gumshoe", scraping chewing gum off pavements, who made a fortune with his ITV backed - they spotted a great story - Exposure on a dead man, rejected by the BBC for the very responsible reason that it was a pack of sensationalist lies, concocted to make a lot of money from a corpse.

You won't find the truth about this elsewhere in media, which sensibly does not believe in shitting on its own doorstep.

But you will find much more detail about the 2015 arrest, publicity and 2018 trial in my book GUILTY, available in all good bookstores and, of course, through Amazon, both as a paperback and as an E book, complete with photos.

80
That's All Folks!

The appalling Williams Thomas was involved only in the very early stages of my 2000 crucifixion, as one of the junior plods sent to interview the liar Kirk McIntyre, who had been inspired by publicist Max Clifford ("thank you so much Max for making this happen" or words to that effect, in a letter sent to the PR person and pervert by the abominable Surrey cop DCI Brian Marjoram after my conviction in 2002) to make false claims against me in the year 2000. I sound like Pulp. Not, I hasten to add, Pulp Fiction.

More about the ghastly Williams Thomas and the horrid Marjoram, now retired ignominiously, after failing to find Milly Dowler's killer, elsewhere.

But when the Savile exposure exploded, leading eventually to the arrest and conviction of others, including, ironically Max Clifford, Surrey Police, or some senior deadhead in their ranks, decided it would be great kudos for the failing force to get another high profile scalp and, since the only celebrity they had succeeding in trapping over the previous two decades had been Jonathan King, why not have a second bite at that juicy cherry?

They had failed, before me, with attempts at both Mick Hucknall of Simply Red and Paul Weller of The Jam - read elsewhere, or Google, if you must.

It took me ages to discover the real reasons for my

2001 prosecution, which is why so much is missing from earlier accounts. Essentially it appears that it was a political manoeuvre by Max Clifford, on behalf of clients working for EMI at the time, to sabotage my Global Chairmanship of the Corporation, which I had accepted on a ten year contract at £5 million a year; a decent sum even back then.

But some information only emerged during this fresh 2015 attempt to prosecute me, which not only failed dismally but enabled me to get access to documents from 15 years earlier, which explained a lot. My defence in 2018 was on Legal Aid, by the way, whereas in 2001 it had cost me a million pounds and was wasted; the most expensive lawyers are often NOT the best; those prepared to work at a low rate because they believe in your innocence are far better and work harder - see GUILTY.

The hysteria after the Savile media explosion, leading, naturally, to no legal cases against his estate whatsoever, had many effects. The millions he had left in his will to Leeds Hospital, in order to build a wing specialising in heart problems, particularly for children, was instead given to lawyers and media tricksters with a few thousand filtering down to the odd false accuser.

One lady, I remember, said in the report conducted by the NHS that she had met Savile in a hospital car park, where he had raped her in front of dozens of drivers. She

80
That's All Folks!

was given hundreds of pounds for the distress caused. And a few sick children died instead. Who cares? Certainly not the media or its masters, us, the public.

The ex plod Mark Williams Thomas, henceforth referred to as MWT, was exposed during my 2018 trial as having tried to obtain the names and contact details of my false accusers in 2001 and, after succeeding, had tried to sell them to the newspapers - in secret, since he had, by then, left the police. HHJ Taylor heavily criticised him, and his behaviour assisted in gaining my acquittals, as you can read in her judgement.

One thing I cannot prove, but suspect, is that he was the anonymous caller to my defence team in 2001, offering the silence and withdrawal of my five false accusers for £5000 each, a total of £25,000 of which, I'm sure, the caller would have kept a hefty chunk.

He's done rather well since, has MWT, though mainly associated with failed attempts at high profile media investigations. The stories I've been told - most of which, sadly, I cannot repeat. But some of which you can read if you Google his name.

Anyway, the Merseyside police force, for some reason, was taken on to examine the 2001 investigation - Operation Arundel. They concluded, correctly, that it had been disastrously inept and had both failed false accusers - oops sorry, victims - and me. Which I knew already.

JONATHAN KING

So Operation Ravine was launched - an attempt by Surrey Police to repeat the Arundel success. It proved, also, to repeat the Arundel failures, leading to several cops losing their jobs, three innocent people dying, as described in my book GUILTY, an abject apology from Surrey Police though not from the useless Police and Crime Commissioner for Surrey, David Munro, who was perfectly happy for Surrey citizens to die, as long as the reputation of his force remained unblemished.

He was voted out of office later, partly due to the revelations in my book Not A Knee On The Neck, which is still available as an E-Book though no longer in print, due to one of the incompetent officers involved threatening to sue me unless I withdrew future print attempts. It does not show her up in a good light.

This chapter is meant to show, in a few cases, how fake claims can be made and can even result in convictions and deaths of innocent people. By providing detailed examples of dishonesty and media exaggeration, I hope to shine a searchlight on the rapidly expanding world of False Allegations. It is the growing crime of the Century. For revenge or sympathy or custody of children or large amounts of cash - who wouldn't lie for tens of thousands of non-taxable money? Or even, often, genuine belief, as memories are affected by time and media coverage.

So read these cases. The names have been redacted,

80
That's All Folks!

although all claims failed, and imagine how you would cope if they happened to you. Your details may be different, but each has aspects which can be translated to other situations. Some may be recreations of imaginary incidents, some confusion, often drugs or drink inspired, some are simply lies and some are adapted truths. In all cases lessons can be learned.

FAILED ATTEMPT ONE...
The **Claridges** case.
I had met Curler (my nickname for the curly haired kid) when he worked as a junior waiter at Claridges. Another friend introduced him to me, knowing I was bi-sexual and that Curler provided services to wealthy clients at the hotel. I immediately liked him - an Artful Dodger type character.

A charming, bubbly, cheeky character. No wonder his twinkly smile attracted potential clients. But not in a million years would I have been interested in hiring him for any kind of sex. ONE - I have never paid for sex; I want the partner to want it and to enjoy it, not for financial reasons. TWO - you never knew what you could catch from promiscuous people in those days. THREE - it would damage my self esteem thinking I had to PAY someone to have sex with me.

Credit where due, Curler never pushed it. Before the

JONATHAN KING

2018 trial my QC asked the Judge, in Legal Argument, if we could question him on his past as a rent boy. The Judge asked whether we had proof of that. "No", we admitted, "only what he had told me". So she refused our request.

During the trial, however, in cross examination, he boasted that he "had made £500 a week at Claridges" as a young teenager. That's £2000 a week in today's money. £100,000 a year as a junior waiter? Clearly Room Service meant something more than just food and drink. HHJ Taylor caught my eye. So did one of the jurors.

Curler had claimed to have been 14 when he worked at the hotel and also when he had met me. We had witnesses from Claridges who said that never would someone have been hired by the hotel at that age. He swore, many times in his 2018 statement and before, when he had made his first claim after my conviction, in 2002 - he later claimed it was in 2001, before my trial; a lie - that he had been introduced to me by our mutual friend AFTER seeing two movies, both of which police established had not been shown in the UK at all until **after** he was 16.

His original 2002 claim, which had been rejected by Surrey Police at the time, was contradicted by so many of his 2018 claims that he said, in court, they had made his earlier claims up. Surrey Police had to produce

80
That's All Folks!

evidence that he had been read and signed his statement **line by line** in 2002 as he was virtually incapable of reading or writing.

His younger sister had told police in 2013, when questioned about their father's possible rapes during another investigation, that Curler had raped her "numerous times when she was 12 and he was 20". She later retracted her claims - but only after she had signed her sworn statement.

She also gave evidence that Curler had told their father that his claims against me from 2002 had been lies and that the father SEAN had replied "if I go down, you're going down with me". Sean had died from cancer a few months later; as a result the case against him was never taken to court.

All this evidence was obtained in researching Curler's claims. As a result the sister was rejected by the CPS as a witness in the 2018 trial, after they had originally included her as a vital witness. Other relatives, including Curler's ex wife, decided not to turn up at the trial, not wishing to perjure themselves.

His only trial witness, a friend from his school days, was sweet, supportive but knew nothing about any contact between him and me except to say, in her police statement, that many lads she knew in the area, at the time, were rent boys.

JONATHAN KING

The Artful Dodger had his claims rejected. I still like him. During his cross examination, at one point, he looked at me, smiled and winked. Two jurors spotted this and smiled at me too. How can you dislike someone so brazen?

FAILED ATTEMPT TWO...
In the 1970s one of my discoveries, GENESIS, had become quite successful.

In a shop somewhere two lads were buying cigarettes and Special Brew strong lager. One approached me and asked if I was Jonathan King. He said he was a huge fan of Genesis, as was his father, who was dying with terminal cancer. He asked me, as a favour, if the next time I was in Birmingham, where they lived, I would visit his Dad. "It would make his day".

So I did, some weeks later. His father PETER turned out not to be a Genesis fan at all but was fascinated by me, especially by the fact that, after my first hit in 1965, I had turned down huge offers to tour and had remained at Cambridge University to complete my studies and get my Master of Arts degree. I valued education. And that, despite being a "pop star", I neither drank nor did drugs.

He felt his son, who I shall call JJ, was "going off the rails" and asked me if I would keep in touch with him and make sure he completed his education, going to college.

80
That's All Folks!

He begged me to take his wife Anne, his older sister, who I had not met, and JJ out to "a really posh restaurant in London" some months after he had passed away, officially to toast to his memory but actually to consolidate my relationship with JJ so I could make sure he didn't "go off the rails completely".

Anne was aware of this, though very much humoured him, winking at me. But that did eventually happen, after his death some months later. She contacted me and I booked a table at Le Gavroche, London's "poshest" and most expensive restaurant off Sloane Square, where we had a lovely meal, spending most of the time discussing JJ's future education.

I kept in touch with JJ, who turned out to be a bit of a monster, requesting all kinds of things, once meeting the man who ran my label UK Records in the 70s, Clive Selwood. Clive had run John Peel's label Dandelion and JJ, by then at college, reckoned he must surely have contacts to dealers from whom he could get drugs to sell to his friends at Uni. Dandelion was quite a "hippy" label. Clive warned me "this guy is trouble - drop him". But when I told him the full story about his father he understood, and respected me for keeping my word.

I got JJ tickets to concerts and festivals, repaid by him and his friends giving out hundreds of leaflets and pamphlets at the events, promoting our products. I was given updates on his education - he did, indeed, finish college. I even dragged myself up to Birmingham for his 21st birthday party, after he begged me again and again to do so, always using my promise to his father as a reason.

"Please wear the multi coloured wig you wore on Top of the Pops" he moaned, although it had been in mothballs for years. I put it on in the car outside his house, went in for about ten minutes, allowed dozens of "selfies", gave him a crate of champagne and left, driving all the way back down to London. I even listened to his step brother's awful demo tape when his mother remarried, which JJ forced me to do, after promising his step father that "nothing to do with sex or drugs has ever, and will never, happened".

I lost touch with JJ. Even during all the publicity of my arrest and conviction in 2001 he failed to contact me. Significantly he also, despite numerous visits to doctors and therapists in the last century, never made any complaints about me. Even in 2015, when I was arrested again in a blaze of publicity, nothing. Then, in 2018, when my upcoming trial was announced, he went to the police with false allegations about me.

We found numerous contradictions and lies in his statement. Clive Selwood was not just prepared but desperate to come to court to give evidence against him. So were previous girlfriends and relatives, some of whom

80
That's All Folks!

gave statements which, again, showed him to be fundamentally dishonest or, at best, mistaken.

In the end, none of it was needed. HHJ Taylor, having seen all the evidence and heard some of the witnesses, not only stopped the trial but refused the CPS request for a retrial which the CPS, knowing the truth, accepted.

Moral: never make claims off the top of your head, based on true facts, that can easily be disproved, especially when you're an alcoholic and a drug addict.

FAILED ATTEMPT THREE...
Decades ago, in the early 1980s - it was a glorious summer day and my friend Ronnie Remnant suggested we go to an outdoor swimming pool for the day. He lived in Walton-On-Thames, as did many other friends. Unfortunately the pool in Surbiton had closed, which we did not know at the time.

In Surbiton we had stopped to ask a young lad the way to the pool and he told us it was shut. Cheekily, he asked for a lift, as we were in my Rolls Royce, back to his home. Ronnie jumped out and got into the back of the car. The boy turned out to be 17, he said, and was very attractive, very handsome and very friendly. I asked if he fancied a drink and a chat. We stopped at an off licence, Ronnie went in and bought two cold beers for him and the lad, and a bitter lemon for me. Then we parked and talked for ten minutes.

It turned out he was an orphan in a care home. He had no idea who I was, so I showed him an interview spread I had just done in Penthouse Magazine. I made it clear I'd like to see him again; he definitely seemed keen and I gave him my phone number. We dropped him off at his home and Ronnie and I went back to the Walton pool, which was, sadly, inside, but better than nothing on this hot, sunny day.

"Don't have anything more to do with him, JK", advised Ronnie. "He's only after money".

But a couple of days later my phone rang. It was the boy. Eager to meet up again. As indeed was I.

Aware of Ronnie's reservation, instead of the Rolls I went down in my little blue TR7. Pulling onto the drive way I saw the boy with another older, larger friend sitting on the steps. I pulled up several yards away, near the EXIT, and locked both doors, putting the passenger door window down a little, leaving the engine running, in neutral gear.

As I feared, only the large friend came over to the car. Smiling sweetly he bent down and said the boy was very nervous about coming with me but if I gave him £50 for himself and £50 for the boy, he thought he could persuade him.

I drove off without exchanging a word. He kicked out

80
That's All Folks!

at the car. I never heard another word from either of them until…

In 2000, after my arrest was all over the papers, the boy went to police with an exaggerated tale. They spoke to his friend who contradicted many of the boy's stories. In legal argument, before the 2001 trial, all his claims were dismissed as fantasy. His allegation was dropped.

So that was that - until 2015 when, finding that almost nobody replied to the advert on the front pages of all the nationals, Surrey Police, desperate to find "victims", tracked down the man, now living in Australia, and asked him if he'd like to revise his claims.

"Oh yes", he said. There could be money in it.

Ronnie had been right, all those years ago. Seeing all the evidence HHJ Taylor, realising the truth, refused to allow the CPS a retrial.

FAILED ATTEMPT FOUR…
One of the very few "new" False Accusers who came forward after my 2015 arrest was Davey Boy who we'll call DB.

DB claimed to have been raped by me in 1970 when he was 15. However his own evidence proved he would have been at least 16 when he met me, IF he had met me.

A totally imaginary encounter that would never have happened, but that was quite hard to disprove from 1970.

JONATHAN KING

Due to the fact that neither could proof or evidence of abuse exist, I would have thought it impossible for charges to be brought. But as the fumbling, collapsing Operation Ravine showed, for lack of anything else it was considered acceptable until, after his cross examination, the trial collapsed, jurors gave Not Guilty verdicts and Judge Taylor forbad any retrials.

I had, and still have, no recollection of ever having met him. Sadly I cannot therefore describe the young man from 55 years ago. Clearly a King's Army member - there were thousands - all ages, all genders. However my friend Noel Keane remembered him, months after the failed trial result, because he had and still has a very memorable surname. Noel didn't remember much except the name, the restaurant in which we had a meal, after which the boy had been sent home in a taxi and our journey then had continued onto the Cromwellian nightclub to meet up with our mutual friend, DJ Kenny Everett.

The man's claims were riddled with inaccuracies that made me aware they were clearly 95% false. He said I drove him in my mini - I've never owned nor driven a mini - my legs are too long - to my flat on the second floor of an apartment building. But I lived in a house and still do. He said the apartment had views of the Park, which, in reality, you cannot see, except on Google Maps. He claimed that I gave him money for a taxi home

80
That's All Folks!

whereas in the 1970s I always used my Owner Driver Radio Taxi Service ODRTS account - number 007 - and never had cash for taxis, which were tax deductible. He boasted to journalist Karen Warner years later in 1991, Aberdeen, that he'd been lead singer with The Weathermen in his good friend Jonathan King's group on Top of the Pops. Not a rapist. A friend. And told police that, after that one encounter, he'd never had any further contact with me - as he whined in his formal statement "No - why would I have?". We found evidence of future phone calls.

Fundamental, total dishonesty.

Just a few examples of falsehoods, often gleaned from media coverage and the new, wonderful asset for false accusers, the INTERNET.

I always remember the vile Carl Beech claiming that Sir Edward Heath had sailed a yacht, before he ever did, and conducted an orchestra, before he even acquired a baton. Liars are often bad liars who don't research dates or facts thoroughly enough.

So protect yourself, if you're ever accused, which is quite likely in this century, especially if you make money or get fame, by examining in detail every single word of the "victim's" statements and you will find error after error.

As I've said, often believed by the accuser because

memory is such a faulty thing, adapting itself over time. And the nuances can be so subtle. A girl may have become pregnant and had a child by some boyfriend or man. The child may now be dead. The man likewise. In memory he becomes a very wealthy, often famous, usually handsome but always innocent celebrity.

"I met him once" can easily become "I met him several times". Or "she flirted with me" can become "she had sex with me". Especially after Harvey Weinstein or Jeffrey Epstein or Puff Daddy or R Kelly or Jimmy Savile type revelations getting headlines. Research some facts; some dates. In 1987 she toured Australia. Stayed in the Southern Cross Hotel in Melbourne. Played a gig on April 1st. There is money in it. Lawyers will convince you. Police will support you - ordered to say "You will be believed - even if you are lying" by Keir Starmer when he was DPP.

Just to be clear - I believe that, in the past, many genuine victims were not believed when they should have been. But we've gone the other way. Now they are ALL believed - which is often unwise, as there are some people prepared to lie for cash reward. And these days many even become convinced by their own exaggerations.

Most of all - MEDIA will back you. Improve your photos.

"Can I have a selfie please with your arm around me

80
That's All Folks!

for my Mum?".

Enhance the telling of your tale. Pay you.

And now, worst of all, the Judicial System will find your "attacker" guilty. And after that - no contest; cash all the way to the bank.

Your expensive lawyers will urge you to pay off the "victims" to avoid a trial and the inevitable conviction. Those impressed by multi million dollar payments forget that £12 million, to some very wealthy people, is £12 to you and I.

Karma nearly always kicks in though. False accusers are often found dead years later, sometimes by their own hands. In vast mansions which are empty, apart from the accuser and servants - families and friends desert the liars when they find out the truth, no matter how wealthy they may be. Guilt kicks in. The self persuasiveness eats away at the soul like acid or bile - they may have convinced themselves but not really, not deeply, not honestly. Many have strokes. The past of False Accusers is littered with bodies - rarely reported or revealed.

It's a double edged sword, False Allegations. A dangerous weapon to play with, sharper than you imagine, with a tendency to turn upon the bearer.

JONATHAN KING

Chapter 12

HELMI, RUPERT MURDOCH, PIERS MORGAN, PRINCE ANDREW

One of the pleasures of rereading the earlier tomes of this three volume autobiography is finding mentions or stories I'd forgotten about. In 70 FFFY I read the story about my Tunisian young friend as an example of how we should all pursue our dreams. His was being a professional diver. Not to do what society told us to do. Weeks after 70 was published, Helmi was arrested for murder. He's still in prison.

A handsome, gentle boy with a fantastic body, as swimmers and divers often have - just look at Tom Daley. In fact Helmi looked a bit like Daley, as you can see from his photo in 70. His father had either died or separated from his Mother, who I met several times. Dad had been a professional footballer in one of the many second division teams - football is very popular in North Africa, as we've recently seen during Morocco's spectacular

80
That's All Folks!

World Cup run of success. I was in Morocco for all of that - a very exciting time, wearing my Moroccan T Shirts and being adopted by all the locals.

As I say in the previous story, I persuaded Helmi to go for a job as the diver on one of the many tourist boats in Tunis - he was hugely popular, well paid, got many tips, which were often coins thrown into the sea to be fetched and kept. Everyone loved him. He was sweet, helpful, genuine, kind.

The only problem, and I blame myself, was that he liked a drink. In Tunisia there are shops that sell alcohol, mainly to tourists. Often, like Morocco, the shops are connected to the big supermarket chains, but tucked away behind the main stores, catering to us non Muslim visitors but often with many Muslim clients who do not believe in strictly obeying the religious rules. Just like Christianity - there are, believe it or not, millions of gay Christians.

A couple of times Helmi asked me to buy him a bottle of whisky. I warned him this was not good for him health wise - like smoking, which he and most teenage Tunisians did and probably still do. Especially as a diver. "Protect your lungs" I said. But addiction is hard to beat when you're a teenager and all your friends are indulging. So when I left Tunisia, about fifteen years ago, Helmi asked me to buy him a bottle so they could celebrate my leaving.

Which I did. He was 18 or 19; old enough to make up his own mind.

It appears that he and his cousin, similar age, got very drunk, had an argument, probably about a girl, as so many teenage arguments are, after which Helmi stabbed and killed his cousin. He has been locked away for life, despite numerous efforts by me through lawyers and others to get him released.

A wasted life. So sad.

I've made so many friends during my trips abroad - it's one of my great pleasures and I noticed that, in the past two volumes, I never mentioned my encounter with **Rupert Murdoch**.

In the 1980s I wrote a weekly page in The Sun newspaper called Bizarre USA. Taken on by the brilliant Editor Kelvin McKenzie, I reported from America on celebrities and curiosities I encountered on my travels, both whilst recording Entertainment USA and on other trips. Remember, I'd converted my New York office for UK Records into an apartment where The Bean and I lived - I travelled to and from London every month, often on Concorde - I was their most flown passenger, had my A1 seat always allocated due to my long legs and later, when I couldn't afford Business Class flights, I was automatically upgraded every time, sometimes from the cheapest, restricted economy tickets.

80
That's All Folks!

The Sun was huge at the time, and my weekly page was massively popular. I remember once, in a traffic jam, seeing the taxi driver in the car in front of me open The Sun, turn to my page, prop it up against the steering wheel and read my words whilst I watched from behind.

The paper was by far the biggest seller in the UK - millions more than the others. The Mirror was then 2nd and The Mail was 3rd.

One Concorde journey, on the way from London to New York, in the luxury lounge, there was Rupert Murdoch and his wife, then the blonde Australian novelist. I quietly approached him and said, "Mr Murdoch, you don't know me but I write a column in one of your publications".

"Best thing in the fucking paper", he replied.

I like this man, I thought.

On the plane, he left his wife sleeping and came and sat next to me for the entire flight. A charming, erudite, attractive man. Funny, intelligent and excellent company. We swapped numbers, though never used them. Quite clearly ruthless and an excellent businessman.

Funnily enough some years later Robert Maxwell, who owned the Mirror, tried to steal me across to his paper. I refused. I wasn't keen on Maxwell, full of bluster, with his horrible dyed hair and huge paunch. He ended up offering me TEN TIMES my Sun salary which was already a lot and could never understand why I refused.

Piers Morgan, my colleague on Bizarre, went on to edit the Mirror. I discuss Piers elsewhere at length but remember recently, in Cannes during the LIONS festival, which has very much taken over from both Midem (music) and the Film Festival as the one conference to attend, bumping into Piers at breakfast.

"Last time I saw you, we were on a hotel bed together" I said.

Rather nervously, as I was, by then, a Vile Pervert, he raised an eyebrow.

"Philadelphia. Rolling Stones. I taught Dave Hogan how to manufacture a fake laminate so he could get up close to the stage". Hogan was then the top Sun photographer. Piers remembered, roared with laughter and we shared a great Carlton hotel breakfast and many memories. I appreciated the fact that, when he was Editor at the Mirror and I had just been wrongly convicted, he managed to carry my entire hand written letter to him, several pages putting my points across, under the pretext of condemning me - "Vile Pervert justifies his appalling behaviour" - giving me great coverage for my side of the stories.

Piers has had a very successful career since our Sun days but he learned a lot from me. Not just how to make fake laminates. Another journalist who became a friend

80
That's All Folks!

and strong supporter was Bob Woffinden.

This incredible man starting writing for the music paper the New Musical Express but quickly became interested in human rights and miscarriages of justice. Before him Ludovic Kennedy had been the key investigative journalist in the area. I wrote to Kennedy from Belmarsh prison, after my wrongful conviction in 2001, and got back a charming, long, hand written letter saying he'd been very concerned about my trial, felt I had been "stitched up" and was 100% supportive but was now retired and simply too old to get involved in his 80s. He said he hated the adversarial approach of British justice - "it is an invitation to the police to commit perjury, which they frequently do". He died a few years later.

So, through a friend in Maidstone Prison, I approached Bob Woffinden who came in to see me. Bob had managed remarkable successes in the area of changing the law regarding prisoners, including forcing Governments to allow prisoners to speak to journalists - which had opened numerous cases and brought about several quashed convictions and appeals. Google Simms and O'Brien for more information.

He collaborated and worked with Richard Webster, another fantastic writer whose research, like Bob's, was meticulous. If you've never read Webster's Secrets of Bryn

JONATHAN KING

Estyn, you should. You'll never believe a case of false allegation again. There was going to be a TV drama, based on the book which was cancelled due to budget cuts by Channel 4. Produced by Tony Garnett, a first rate director who worked a lot with Ken Loach, like Mike Leigh, one of my heroes. Had it been made, I have no doubt the impact on society would have been similar to that of Mr Bates VS The Post Office on ITV many years later.

Bob was very nice but rightly said that my case would be very hard to dismiss, as I openly and clearly admitted to having broken the law, which I thought was stupid, that said females were able to consent to sex aged 16 but males could only do so, with other males, if they were over 21.

I pointed out to him that the law also said that if both male parties were over 16 and had not made a complaint within 12 months of the act, nobody could any longer be prosecuted. This intrigued him, I think as much as by the fact that I had investigated the law through the Belmarsh prison library as by the law itself. He promised to look into it, and indeed he did.

He was horrified by what he found out. So much so that when he wrote, in 2015, The Nicholas Cases, his book on the ten worst miscarriages of justice in British history over the past 30 years, he included my case as one

80
That's All Folks!

of the ten. The case of Andrew Malkinson, later totally acquitted of rape, was another.

I was actually a bit embarrassed. Surely my silly little case, regarding whether I not I gave someone a consensual wank 50 years ago, was less significant than people still, at the time of writing this, in prison for crimes they did not commit, such as murder? No, said Bob, in many ways your case is the most significant of all, as it really throws a light on police and court behaviour.

The book received rave reviews. The Mail On Sunday praised it to the heavens. In a Google review… "This book relates the stories of English lives that have been destroyed by malfunctioning criminal justice processes. In theory, wrongful conviction should not necessarily ensue from wrongful arrest and charge, but in practice there is a dismal inevitability about it."

By 2016 Bob and I had become close friends. His brother had been diagnosed with asbestos related cancer. Bob told nobody except perhaps his wife that he, too, had played, with his brother, on the site of the asbestos, but was unwilling to mention this whilst his brother underwent treatment in case it deflected attention. After his brother died, Bob asked me if I thought he should go to be tested.

"Under no circumstances", I said. "You have no symptoms, you're perfectly healthy. If you get sick, then by all means go but you are NOT, I repeat NOT, to go otherwise".

He considered my advice and we talked it through several times. But it played on his mind and he could not avoid going to be checked.

He was found to have the same kind of cancer. He had treatment - chemo, which I hate - do not deliberately poison your body unless it is tightly targeted and, often, not even then. The day before he died his wife Anne, who is also a friend, called and said Bob wanted me to visit him. Propped up in bed, hazy with drugs, he kept fading out. "Will you stop dying when I've come all this way to visit you?" I snapped - Anne said it was the first time she'd seen him laugh in ages.

We chatted at length. I held his hand and told him I loved him. I did. He was a genuinely wonderful human being. He assured me that, even if he was dead, he would be with me in court every second of my 2018 trial. I'd been arrested in 2015 to Bob's amazement - "they must be mad" he'd said. He was. I felt him by my side every second I was in the box.

He died at 4.00AM the next morning. He is badly missed.

I should probably reveal here, in the spirit of transparency, that Bob thought Volume One of my autobiography, 65 My Life So Far, was "probably the

80
That's All Folks!

worst written book I've ever read". Despite the fact that it had 5 Editors, he said it was - is still - full of grammatical errors.

"You've had one of the most interesting lives of anybody ever. The book deserved to be better".

He even sent me a huge long list of mistakes, repeats and blemishes, page by page. It must have taken him ages - this was back in 2007. But it was already published and I couldn't be bothered. I leave it to you to judge, in this third volume, whether I'm still "a terrible writer".

Bob was a superb writer. But, far more important, he was an absolutely lovely human being. I miss him every day.

There is however an important moral to be learned from Bob's life. I only hope any police chief or government politician or judge reading this - or, indeed, any media editor - will give thought to the following.

Bob, Richard Webster and indeed Ludovic Kennedy were diligent, forensic researchers. The jobs they did on their projects were exemplary and should have been done by the police or, if not, by the CCRC. They spent hours examining every detail of each case. Quite often, Bob told me, he decided that the perpetrator was indeed guilty, and gave up the case. But he should not have had to do this.

The case of Andrew Malkinson was meticulously examined and Bob was certain he was innocent, long before the DNA evidence emerged. And that was only found when the APPEAL charity, a marvellous organisation to which I urge you to contribute, tracked it down. But the Court of Appeal agreed with Bob. Malkinson should have been referred to them at least a decade earlier, had the CCRC been any good at its job. Which, by the way, is NOT to second guess the Court. They have neither the budget nor the experience and training to do that.

If you read The Nicholas Cases you'll agree that all ten, including mine, thank you very much, warranted an appeal and an acquittal. And the other eight of them are either languishing in prison, innocent of the crimes, or dead.

Frightening.

One of my remaining ambitions in life is, if I win my appeal about the 2001 wrongful conviction, I can sue Surrey Police for the £50 million I would have earned as Global Chairman of EMI and give that money to either an existing organisation, like APPEAL, to hire and train investigators to cope with the thousands of wrong convictions or to start up a similar legal set up for those who, like Malkinson, cannot afford to buy the truth and justice.

But let's look, for a moment, at the recent "scandal" involving Prince Andrew, the King's brother, and the

80
That's All Folks!

allegations against him made by the appalling late Virginia Giuffre.

I know nothing, other than what's been in the media. Precisely as much, I suspect, as you.

Watching Andrew's interview with Emily Maitlis on the BBC, I felt he came across as 85% genuine. My suspicion, and I hasten to add this is only a suspicion, is that he did meet Virginia Roberts, as she then was, when she was 17 and above the legal age of consent in the UK, quite likely that he had consensual sex with her, quite possibly gave her "a little present", and probably posed for a selfie with her, as he would have done with thousands of others. He may not even remember the encounter - one, I suspect, of many. Promiscuity was not only accepted but obligatory decades ago.

And what was she? What was Virginia?

Reading her diaries and her books, it's clear she either WAS abused as a child, and many sadly are, or found, and consented, that "doing stuff" won her affection, kindness, friendship, popularity and even, possibly, funds.

I would guess, as she reached her teens, that she discovered she could earn a lot of money by being a willing prostitute. She came across very wealthy people like Epstein and Trump who may have been delighted to indulge in consensual, legal activities and even to reward such kindness with expensive gifts. Again, I know nothing but I just guess, with 80 years of experience and observations of human life on our planet.

Then she fell in love, got married, deserted her previous life and became a wife, mother and housewife.

However, she became aware that there was potentially a great deal of money to be made, with a little help from enablers, from the False Allegations Industry. And started on the path NOT of lying but of exaggeration - the key, essential talent required. Easy to do and reflecting society and media - always prepared to take, and pay for, great stories.

Fairly soon those close to her, immediate family like husbands and children, started sussing her character. She may, indeed, have become a victim of domestic abuse. But that, either inflated or invented, turned into another element of "a tragic life" except, as, again, is frequent, she knew the truth herself. And that tends to destroy a human being, often leading to an early death. That's what I think happened to Virginia Giuffre ne Roberts.

But I repeat - I know nothing.

80
That's All Folks!

Chapter 13

BOOKS, FILMS, MUSIC AND EVEN ELTON JOHN

One thing was clear after my wrongful conviction in 2001 - life was never going to be the same again. Even if, as I hoped and expected, the Court of Appeal would throw out my conviction and tell me, gravely, that I "leave this court without a stain on your character", no music company would hire me or release my work, however good or commercial it was, and no publication would ever print a word I wrote again.

Indeed I noticed that those "Birthday today" sections in all the papers, which had carried mine on every December 6th since 1965, failed, since 2001, ever to include my name in the lists. Not one. To this day. I am officially a Vile Pervert, and, as such, Persona Non Grata in the print, radio, TV and media worlds.

Fine by me, and inevitable. So I worked out a way to bypass traditional methods of communicating with the world, and increase my already active online presence.

80
That's All Folks!

The Tip Sheet board had been online since the middle 1990s - inspired by my dear friend Julie Gordon and her Velvet Rope forum in America, combined with the print and CD subscription only version - and inspired, in turn, by my dear friends Bill and Janet Gavin in San Francisco, whose The Gavin Report was hugely influential in America. I'd met them in 1965 and we became long term buddies. They even visited me in London.

The moment I emerged from Her Majesty's Luxury Estate in 2005, I took on James, a suggestion from Little Joe who had been one of our great Tip Sheet finds. Called Little Joe after the Bonanza character - he went to Oxford after doing Work Experience at The Tip Sheet and came back afterwards to be Editor of the music magazine. James had been the boyfriend of Joe's girlfriend, now wife's, sister.

I needed someone who was really in touch with the new, online world of downloads and, later, streaming, to sell all our back catalogue by Genesis, 10cc, The Rocky Horror Show, all my hits under pseudonyms and other linked copyrights, and to make sure any future projects got distributed and promoted. And as time went by - my Mum died and many of her duties were taken on by her housekeeper, the wonderful Molly Brown, truly unsinkable, who became my book keeper and organiser for many years - then she too died, partly as a result of the stress caused by Surrey Police raiding her home in 2015, and James took on all her functions.

As well as attending every meeting and every minute of every day of the 2018 trial and all subsequent legal and financial sessions.

I reckoned the way to get my story across was to make a full length online movie, with me playing all 21 roles as no actors would work with a Vile Pervert - even Polanski had problems. I used primitive videos of some old hits and some new music. You can see, watching and listening today how amateur my attempts were - mainly using still shots and the Zoom facility on Final Cut Pro. But I think it works. To a degree.

If you're interested, much more, including photos of me in 21 disguises, are in 65 My Life So Far.

It was great fun to do, cost me almost nothing and was picked up from the dedicated site (www.VilePervert.com) as free to view by all the new streaming services. These - in the past decades - became massive and it has had, so far, almost 20 years later, over **TEN MILLION VIEWS!**

I think some executives and entrepreneurs, watching it fly, mainly because it was free, saw the future. Subscriptions. Profits.

NETFLIX, you owe me a thank you. Like so many.

Apart from being great fun and requiring incredible amounts of imagination to create for almost nothing,

80
That's All Folks!

though it sounds fantastic - those tracks had cost a fortune to make in previous years, the challenges were massive. As the technology developed, with the iPhone becoming a proper camera, I adapted and learned more and more. James played a huge part in all of them, as did my friends Steve Levine - a top producer in his own right, with fantastic studios and Paul Wiffen, an award winning Director, introduced to me by Steve. So the movies are not without professional involvement.

All my films seem to have become cult viewing. All online though we do also have the odd midnight cinema screening, like the films of Andy Warhol or Derek Jarman or Roger Corman, but totally different to all of those, you can see details later here and elsewhere. I'm still doing it - the latest in 2024 was Three Women. Free to view on www.ThreeWomenX.com and everywhere else. The You Tube version alone has had ten thousand views in just a couple of months. I had to grow a beard and moustache for it; totally changed my face; I hated them and was delighted to shave them off.

I've loved making movies and videos. Do it all myself. Write them. Cast them. Direct and produce them. Often even film them and edit them. Thank God for Final Cut Pro.

For The Pink Marble Egg we got an enormous egg strapped to the roof of my Rolls Royce and I drove it down to Cannes for the film festival, where it garnered massive publicity, some praise and many fans - best of all an old man who waved to me as I went down the Corniche and gave me thumbs up - Steven Spielberg.

It all took a huge amount of learning, but as a result it's become an art form and far, far cheaper to do than the Hollywood movie franchises. Also, as a result, they are not very good. They are different and original but only about 60% of what they should be. Like much art.

And much of the joy can be accidental.

One of my favourite parts of Three Women is the police woman. I'd booked one of my regular, superb actresses, who's done lots of work for me in other films - she was starring in the lead role in a West End play and we organised the filming schedule so she could fit it in between shows, rehearsals and so on. Quite tricky.

Then, on the day before filming, she got ill - seriously unable to speak. An understudy had to do the theatre show. Desperate, I asked our makeup and hair girl, Grace Darling Smith - if she could stand in. The poor girl had never acted but agreed. We had to do it line by line, but she is fantastic - her nerves meant she simply said the words flatly, looking bored to tears, exactly the effect I wanted.

My professional actress would have delivered it as a REAL POLICE OFFICER but actually Grace, bored

80
That's All Folks!

and calm, never phased, despite the awful police revelations and instructions, was perfect. It's one of my favourite parts of the movie. The sub text is magnificent.

Mind you, the viewer may never notice. But that and many other marvellous moments (my actors were all brilliant) supplied all the subtle bits I wanted. Just as in the fantastic recent TV series Adolescence, often greatness comes from allowing filming to stray from the script and original plan. Accidental brilliance. I'm sure Van Gogh once spilled some paint and saw it made odd shades of brown. His use of brown is one of the finest aspects of my favourite painter.

And I've been writing books as well as screenplays. The first volume of my autobiography 65 My Life So Far was in hardback - we printed up 500 and put them through the site and Amazon for £20 each. They sold out in a week. The E-Book version is still available and we've now reprinted it, due to demand, in glossy large paperback which is much better for the photos.

Since then not just Vols 2&3 - 70 FFFY and this one - 80 - but various assorted novels and diaries. They all seem to go to a select band of readers - several thousand each time. They don't make me much money, simply covering the costs, but are fun to do and they keep me occupied. I'm a bit of a cult. See You L t.

A friend said "JK I think you'll become very famous

only after you're dead". That's probably true, and goes along with all the other projects in my life.

Again and again I was ahead of my time. So, if your reading this after I'm buried or cremated, I hope you appreciate the effort I've gone through. The thoughts of Chairman King should influence humanity in the next 75 years, for the rest of this rather dodgy century; if humanity has any sense, which I fear it doesn't. Stupid Brexiteers even want to leave the Human Rights body because, they say, we Brits aren't humans.

Toast me with a Bloody King - like a Bloody Mary but with Malibu coconut favoured rum instead of vodka and no tabasco; eat an avocado pear; giggle at my barminess and, for God's sake, learn from my many mistakes.

I've made several new music tracks - again some of the lyrics are in 65. I think my best ever lyric is When Caravaggio Met Michelangelo. I often recreate fresh sounds to fit the films. The fuss my song about Harold Shipman caused in 2007. And The Silver Stoat, my song about Max Clifford, sounds far better now, after history exposed him. Although Max, to give him credit, said my portrayal of him in Vile Pervert: The Musical, was "amazingly accurate".

I can see, from the URLs, that, still, media views every post on every forum (KingOfHits.com) - we get over 10,000 views a day, though far far fewer comments and

80
That's All Folks!

posts these days. People can waffle on with X (Twitter) and Instagram and Facebook and You Tube and TikTok - oh yes - we're on them all and dozens of others - you have to be these days; even in places like China. It is now so easy to spread the word. But so hard to get noticed. Even people with millions of followers mean nothing in the greater scheme of things. You can be massive to a tiny section of fans these days. Bet you can't hum a single BTS tune or quote one word of a Taylor Swift lyric.

The sad fact is that in the 1960s I had lots of energy and imagination; some of that was reflected in my music - my personal favourites are my version of Satisfaction under the name Bubblerock - a small hit, back in the 70s, though it did sell over a million copies; A Very Very Melancholy Man; Hooked on A Feeling (Ooga Chagga)… they had lots of imagination.

But I also came up with great promotion and marketing ideas. I lost that, probably in the 80s when I really moved into television and writing my columns and articles. So now, at 80, I have no idea how to break, promote and expose my products, my thoughts or my art.

And I haven't been able to do it for decades. Even my hits in the late 90s - Who Let The Dogs Out? I Get Knocked Down But I Get Up Again - had to be made, released and broken by others. Neither The Baha Men nor Chumbawamba contributed anywhere near as much to the success of those giant hits as I did - each sold 16 million copies. And 90% of the reasons they caught on were ideas of mine - "Play them in sports stadiums when a player gets knocked down - and then gets up again".

So almost everything I've done since 2001 has sunk without trace. But that doesn't mean it wasn't - isn't - any good. Either artistically or intellectually or commercially. And my friend may be right. I can see re-released smashes and hit movies and chart topping books catching on in the last half of this century.

Novels like Thomas Love Peacock Luv Tom, Beware The Monkey Man and Don't Go In may be future studies for great works in Universities. You don't have to crack it when you're alive. Just ask the ghost of Vincent Van Gogh, my favourite painter, unappreciated during his lifetime. And we found, during the massive spring clean inspired by the search for stuff - three old works of mine, ripe for adapting and republishing.

Animal Farm - The Next Chapter - inspired by the events in Russia since Orwell's master work, had almost been published when written in the late 1990's. But copyright laws had just been expanded to 75 years. The original was first published in 1945. Now - 80 years later, like me - my Daddy knew Orwell - it is ripe for publishing, after a bit of updating; events have moved forward in Russia, oops, Animal Farm - and it would

80
That's All Folks!

make a superb AI movie. We're spreading the rumour that both Putin and Trump have bought copies. They are both included in the book.

As Pope Francis died - I thought he was a good Pope - the best since John Paul II - I found my short story **The Polish Boy And The Pope**, which I'd sent to John Paul when he was appointed in 1973, and received a glowing letter of thanks, giving me, and it, his blessing. So that has now been put out again as an E Book.

The illustrations were done by my friend Jack Oliver, who also did the drawings for **The Adventures Of Tim**. That requires hefty improvement and bringing into this century, but will come out in due course. All great works for future generations. Wait and see. I probably won't be around to notice, unless I've returned, hopefully as my favourite animal, a tiger. Can tigers read? I think they are stunningly beautiful so, really, what else matters? As in so much in life - that superficial impact is, ultimately, all that concerns us.

And it's not just great works that increase in worth. A friend specialises in selling online old vinyl, the more obscure the better. As I've got older I've found funds drying up, especially when health and legal costs mount, and he suggested selling off my enormous mountain of 60s and 70s vinyl. By the 80s most promotion stuff, sent to me for radio, TV and column critiques, were given to charities. I favoured Shelter and Medecins Sans Frontieres. But I still had literally thousands of older vinyl singles and albums stored away.

He's managing to get seriously hefty four figure sums each month for these tacky old, dusty bits and pieces. Acetates by groups like The Beatles fetch a fortune. They were cut, not pressed, so took as long as each track was - only a few dozen were made for group members, producers and engineers to check before the final master went off to be pressed. I, of course, had hundreds of these.

And my friend, being an expert, could pick up some obscure 7 inchers and gasp "before Jimmy Page was in Led Zeppelin - worth a fortune!". Since Jimmy played acoustic guitar on Everyone's Gone To The Moon as a session musician, such things meant little to me.

Way back in the 1970s I was not just a friend to Top of the Pops but, since being the first booking on the first London show in 1965, a regular in their offices, seeing the new charts coming in and much relied upon, as I knew every release and was very good at picking future hits. And, especially, I was honest - if I was in any way connected to a release I told them.

My phone rang. It was Madeleine Bell, a brilliant session singer and, later, an artiste in her own right. "You have influence with Top of the Pops, don't you?", she said.

80
That's All Folks!

"Yes".

"You must get this new release on - it's by Reg, you know, the little gay piano player with John's band. He's calling himself Elton John these days".

She sent it over by messenger. She had nothing to gain - I don't think she was even on it - she just loved it. So did I. It was called Your Song.

I called the Producer, another friend - Mel Cornish. "You must book this guy". He did, on the spot.

Just another of the many acetates now cherished by some collector somewhere. I've got the memory. Both Madeleine and Elton are still with us, at the time of writing.

Chapter 14

THE CRIME OF THE CENTURY

I first became aware of the crime of the century in 2000 when I was arrested, questioned, charged and eventually convicted of crimes that had never taken place, that there was no evidence that they had ever taken place and that would make a lot of money for a lot of dishonest - and honest - people.

The FALSE ALLEGATIONS INDUSTRY
At a meeting in the House of Commons, I confronted Peter Garsden. The gathering had been organised by Ronnie Campbell MP, a delightful old Geordie who had been discovered as the long lost brother of the Boss of Inside Time, Eric McGraw.

Eric's monthly paper went out free to all prisoners. It had been founded by the mighty Lord Longford, one of my heroes. In it I wrote a regular column.

Garsden, a lawyer, was one of the first to make a fortune from this business. Though, to give him credit, he described it as "the historical sex abuse exposure

80
That's All Folks!

industry". As he said to me in front of Jonathan Aitken, also attending the meeting, "this is a goldmine".

It keeps on growing. Every time you see "a great story" involving a celebrity or wealthy superstar or a top politician or media mogul or top cop or virtually anybody, bear this in mind.

Probably the most high profile victim so far has been Prince Andrew. Twelve million quid which, let's be blunt, is next to nothing to him, for something that never happened or, if it did, was perfectly legal. Consensual sexual contact with a hooker aged over 16. But, when assisted by clever lawyers, media experts, often police and judges - not required in his case - a fortune made by all concerned.

I saw it in 2000. If this could happen to me, it could happen to many others, unless and until the law was changed and the media became morally responsible. Some chance.

Karma kicked in as far as my case was concerned, with several participants. Max Clifford went to jail, hoist on his own petard, and died there. But also with others. Virginia Giuffre nee Roberts took her own life, totally separated from her family and alone.

I'm not sure what happened to Peter Garsden. He sold his company, or merged it, to Simpson Millar. Which went on to become major representatives to those seeking justice or, at least, compensation for events that may or may not have happened in the past. One of the other firms known for this kind of work was Slater and Gordon. You'll find lawyers linked to these firms connected to many cases - likewise, in America, the mighty Gloria Allred, a legendary attorney in the USA, often willing to represent claimants, though I have no idea how often she agrees to bravely waive any fees.

Let's be fair, many of these legal eagles have no interest in profit but only want to bring justice to poor victims of crime. Many of whom, let's be fair, were unable or unwilling to make complaints when any incidents occurred.

Many of whom genuinely believe they were abused. Again, let's be fair, some of whom may actually have been abused.

None of this chapter applies to them.

But getting back to Garsden, I'm not sure what took place in his life. After many years of successfully championing those who claimed to have been assaulted, fiddled with, raped, seduced, betrayed, taken advantage of or even just insulted or smacked, he seems to have become a victim himself.

Whether or not it was of a false allegation, I have no idea. He was, as a side line, a foster parent - the fantastic, much needed job which could also, though I'm sure it

80
That's All Folks!

wasn't, be useful for "hiding in plain sight", as several of his jailed offenders were. But for whatever reason, Garsden, after commencing a series of "pre-action protocol" letters to me after my 2018 acquittals, left Simpson Millar without any explanation that I can find. I'd love to know more.

One of his close friends and associates was another Peter - Saunders, the founder of a hugely successful and wealthy charity NAPAC, the organisation for adults abused in childhood, which he often represented in the media.

Saunders made several negative comments about my case, after my wrongful conviction in 2001, so I was aware of him and examined him closely.

When the Carl Beech case exploded - Google him - the man who claimed Sir Edward Heath and others had abused him; currently doing an 18 year prison sentence - Saunders popped up on telly justifying his close connection to the man, who had been involved with not only NAPAC but several other charities and abuse organisations. I was deeply offended when I saw Saunders on TV saying that false claims of sex abuse, such as Beech's, were "vanishingly rare". They are not. They are the majority.

I investigated him.

And found that some other online investigators had

spotted gaps and contradictions in his claims of past abuse. Much of this is carried in his own explanation of his life, available via Amazon, called The Truth. It appears, however, to be far from the truth.

I mention all this only as an example of all the other areas of criminality involved in the False Allegations Industry. I discuss the police elsewhere - reputations made, budgets increased, promotions - oh, there are huge advantages for bent cops to win cases. Police should, surely, be balanced. Neither on one side nor the other. But, more often than not, they obey the guide "You will be believed". No. Not if you are lying. You will be believed if you are telling the truth. But it's not just cops.

I was intrigued to find that Saunders, in one of his many high profile positions as "spokesperson" for the sex abuse "survivors" (he was on the IICSA, for example), had been on the Committee set up by Pope Francis to examine the appalling situation of child abuse by church members. Many priests, bishops, vicars and clergymen had been found guilty of crimes, often against small children, such as choirboys.

Francis, a good man and one of the finest Popes, was determined to root out the evils in the Catholic Church.

But in the selfie, provided online by Saunders, it looked very much to me like the selfie taken of Bob Geldof, decades earlier, with Mother Teresa, when she

80
That's All Folks!

was clearly not entirely comfortable with the Live Aid King. The words "garlic" and "vampires" spring to mind. Francis looks distinctly uncomfortable with Peter Saunders.

I soon discovered why. Saunders was later removed from the Vatican Commission. He put out stories of him quitting but I felt those sounded like a coverup. The Vatican has very many sources. I bet Francis was aware, even before he met Saunders, that there were skeletons in the closet. I looked further. Fortunately I have an army of information providers - The King's Army still exists, though very different today. It even includes The Vatican.

As I said above - The Truth seems far from the truth, compared to the official police statement and interview which he signed as the truth at the time. Which only a few people can know about officially, but those few, including his son Greg, 19 at the time and aware of the truth, must find deeply disturbing. In his response to the charge of taking advantage of an adult vulnerable victim of sex abuse, he resorted to one of the many, or "vanishingly rare", excuses made by other perpetrators - VICTIM BLAMING.

Anyway, just another example of an area of huge profits from the False Allegations Industry. I wonder whether he is still making millions from the charity, though now officially no longer connected to it. That could be incorrect and I would never dream of suggesting any such thing. I'm sure that if anything was going on, it would anyway be concealed such as by royalties being paid to the wife - that sort of trick.

But let me describe what this rapidly expanding crime of the 21st Century is. It's been around for years as blackmail, extortion and other petty crimes. Indeed the appalling Mark Williams Thomas, mentioned several times here and elsewhere, was once accused and prosecuted for blackmail - attempting to extort cash from a funeral parlour, I believe. Burying several bodies in the same coffin. He was acquitted on all charges - this was back in the last century. Walked free without a stain on his character. Unblemished. A fine, moral, upstanding man.

Excuse me whilst I'm sick.

As new technology developed and we saw the Internet take over, providing evidence for potential blackmailers like Carl Beech - "look up Sir Edward Heath Prime Minister - find "evidence" like his conducting orchestras and sailing ships - adapt to suit allegations - go to police or a publicist who will tell you, first, to go to the police; cry a lot; buried memories; give details of past homes and places, sobbing throughout" - but also for the enablers, men and women who encourage, assist, spend money obtaining "evidence" (I'm sorry I keep putting "evidence" and "proof" in inverted commas, must stop

80
That's All Folks!

doing that) and take a hefty percentage of any award or compensation payment or media interview fee or settlement sum - "go away, please, here's lots of money but a mere tiny percentage of what's being demanded in your modern, cut from newspapers, blackmail note" - that the "victim" may win.

I call it **USING THE LAW TO BREAK THE LAW**

It went on a lot in the past, with lawyers usually attacking dead people or their estates - faced by the enormous costs of defending these spurious cases, and attacked by truly vicious and nasty legal letters, no longer cut from newspapers, most estates, not having expected much money from their deceased family or friends, give way very quickly and settle for a hefty deduction from their already depleted, tax wise, inheritance.

My friend, top barrister and KC Daniel Janner, son of Greville Janner MP, a victim of false accusers when alive, suffered from this after his father's death - as have many - but refused to settle and then lawyers concerned dropped their claims.

The problem is - most other lawyers, some on the defence side, know these cases can be a goldmine, as Garsden said in 2005, for them too. Both solicitors and KCs love a civil case. Lots of money - legal aid cannot apply, with its derisively low rates of pay; they can and do charge a fortune - I gather Kevin Spacey has had to sell his house to cover their fees.

Which brings me to the second crime - against those convicted who are languishing in jail; often their wives, husbands, children have to sell the family home to cover the costs of defending civil cases. Out on the streets.

At least the convicted criminals, many of whom are innocent - read Bob Woffinden's The Nicholas Cases - the tip of the iceberg, have roofs over their heads, three meals a day, medical care.

Again, the enablers win. Oh, the False Accusers or, in a few cases, genuine victims get a bit. But the real winners are the enablers.

Which brings me to my third example - those acquitted in a Court of Law - like actor Kevin Spacey. And myself. This is shocking. Absolutely shocking. Lawyers, Judges, Police, Media are all locked in a massive collusion to commit crimes.

The law is set up, in civil cases, to allow those wrongly abused, by the law "getting it wrong", to pursue the perceived perpetrators, be it in murder, rape, fraud or violence. If the villain has escaped justice they can still be prosecuted in the civil court system.

But to do so on either side costs a fortune. Fortunately the law allows fine, brave upstanding lawyers to represent clients on a No Win No Fee basis, assuring them it needs far less evidence in a civil case and telling them, for a large

80
That's All Folks!

deduction (sometimes as much as 50%) they will represent them, take on all the massive or minuscule costs and bring them a fortune.

Fair enough, you will say; if the poor victim cannot afford justice, the system should let them get it, by using generous, fine, upstanding honest lawyers prepared to obtain it for them.

Fine in principle. Except that a loophole can be used. Dishonest liars or even the genuinely convinced, and memory can be a very faulty faculty, especially when similar situations are inflated and coloured up in regular news coverage. Wives wanting custody of children. Revenge Seekers. Attention Seekers. And those few innocent, honourable people who simply find the idea attractive of making a few thousand tax free quid at no risk to themselves,.

Oh beware of those traitorous tempters who offer you money for nothing.

QOCS. Qualified One-Way Cost Shifting.

This is a legal term used in litigation. It's a rule that limits the responsibility of a losing claimant in a lawsuit to have to return the legal costs of the winning party. This rule is used to protect the claimant from paying the winning party's expenses, with some exceptions. Essentially, this meant that if a claimant lost a court case, they would be relatively protected from having to pay the defendant's legal fees, whereas if a defendant lost, they would likely have had to pay the claimant's legal fees.

Until April 2023 this meant that a defendant's costs could not be claimed back from the claimant, if the case was lost. And those costs can be enormous. Extraordinary, I'm sure you will agree. How on earth such a legal rule ever existed is beyond comprehension. Surely someone, somewhere worked it out that this was a charter for blackmailers and extortionists.

Bent lawyers often did not inform their "clients", who, in No Win No Fee cases were not actually clients, of the risk this process might entail. A "client" might find themselves liable for costs, mounting to hundreds of thousands of pounds, if the trial went against them.

Especially if - and this applied even before the QOCS changes in April 2023 - they and/or their claims were proved fundamentally dishonest. This could be if, for example, they had claimed to being younger than they were, especially if their claims depended on consensual acts before the age of 16. Consensual acts after the age of 16 are now, in this liberated and sensible century, not only acceptable but legal.

If, for example, family members or friends or other witnesses contradicted basic details of claims made. If, for example, there was evidence that the claimants had deliberately lied or even were genuinely confused. If, for

80
That's All Folks!

example, they had appeared in court or even had been found guilty of crimes of dishonesty, no matter how trivial or how long ago.

When told of this, many clients, knowing they had lied or exaggerated or been mistaken in sworn statements given on oath, might wish to pull out.

Some bent lawyers, not wishing to lose all their hard work and investment, would not want this. Especially if they know that a potential victim of the False Allegations Industry might try to claim that No Win No Fee cases meant that the lawyers, if informed of evidence regarding fundamental dishonesty by their clients, could be held responsible for costs and damages of attempted extortion from an innocent person or a guilty one, come to that.

Remember, in the good old days, that it didn't matter if a blackmail victim was innocent or guilty - they could not, and should not, be blackmailed. Blackmail was a crime. Extortion was a crime.

The problem mentioned above remains true in 2025. Defence lawyers, especially KCs, love civil cases and make a fortune from them. Sometimes they may not mention crucial facts or even let their defendants know about rule changes. The Court system, from Judges downwards, feels, quite rightly, that a system should exist, finding justice for those unable to pay for it. Which opens a loophole, used by criminals. To waste court time, even if it is just in the area of administration.

USING THE LAW TO BREAK THE LAW.

There is a system in place called Mediation, where an independent adjudicator meets with both parties to try and find a mutually agreeable way to solve the problem. They tend to be very good, straight and honest. They tell you about the "worst case scenarios" which will cost you millions - mostly in legal fees if you lose. And "best case scenarios" - what you have spent - wasted - so far, including the substantial mediation costs - but, again, these mediations are slanted towards claimants or their enablers getting "bought off". Never do they say "you could win and get a decent judge who would declare that you should get all your legal costs back from the claimants and, if they cannot afford to pay them, from their lawyers who were working on a No Win No Fee basis, which ought to be called No Win We Pay".

If a falsely accused defendant, found innocent in a Court of Law, wants his or her costs repaid by a dishonest claimant or, more importantly, by the lawyers representing them on No Win No Fee deals, those massive costs MUST be part of a mediated settlement, where the dishonest claimant agrees to drop the charges and to pay back all or most of the defendant's costs.

You'll be wondering - how did bent lawyers get hold

80
That's All Folks!

of contact details for dishonest claimants, to persuade them to go for it in a No Win No Fee way?

We return to Mark Williams Thomas who, after he left Surrey Police under a cloud in 2000, contacted another officer, still on the case, to get such contacts and names of "victims" before the 2001 trial, in order to sell them to the media, as revealed in previously secret documents during the 2018 trial.

The officer concerned refused his demand and reported him to her bosses. But still, somehow, as previously mentioned, the appalling MWT found the details and offered them to the media for a great deal of cash. If it was that easy, one assumes that it would be equally easy for a senior bent cop, having been soundly defeated in a Court of Law and, quite possibly, lambasted by the Judge when she refused to allow any retrials in 2018, to sneak the names and details to a law firm. Nudge nudge, wink wink, say no more. Easy but immoral and, quite possibly, illegal.

Of course this would be unlikely, and impossible if the False Accusers all went to different lawyers, hired them at great expense and were prepared to take the risk of spending a fortune to make a fortune. But if they were all represented by the same firm and the same lawyer - what a co-incidence.

Your Honour.

Chapter 15

SENILITY, ALZHEIMERS, PRISON LIFE AND MR KING

My mum said, as she approached her 90th birthday and we chatted as we always did, she propped up on her pillows in her bed, me perched on a chair next to her - "You don't want to live past 80".

Every part of you started to ache, she explained. Your mind began to go as senility took over. "The 80s are awful. I dread the 90s".

She made it to 91 but in great pain, with ulcers on her feet caused by years of smoking and a wrecked circulation due to the nicotine habit.

She remained sharp as a pin mentally until the very end and not too physically frail, except for the agony of the legs. But she had a point.

I'm nowhere near as bright as I was ten years ago. I'm starting to ache in silly places like shoulders? Who needs aching shoulders? And I keep forgetting things.

What was that I was saying?

80
That's All Folks!

So much so that I requested my Doctor to contact the best senility expert in the United Kingdom to assess whether or not I was senile.

The top, expensive consultant seemed a decent bloke and explained there were three tests he had to do. The first was words and a series of questions. The second was a blood test, thoroughly examining odd things like platelets. What the fuck are platelets? Little plates?

The third was a scan - I can't remember its name. See?

He began by telling me about some fictional woman and her address and said he'd be asking me about her in an hour. Then a series of questions, quite detailed including NAME WORDS BEGINNING WITH P - one minute.

Prostitute, penis, paedophile… he started to laugh uncontrollably. When the minute was up he said "you've actually given me more words than I think there are in the dictionary. Must be your Cambridge education".

"Not at all", I answered, "it's because I'm a pervert with a capital P".

Another was "name Animals". When the minute was up he said "I can only give you 98 out of a hundred - you didn't name any insects".

Insects? Since when have insects been animals? Well, I suppose, as BEES are some of my favourite creatures, I should have remembered them.

At the end of the hour he asked me for the imaginary woman's name and address. I gave them to him.

"You've done remarkably", he said. "Now the blood test".

My blood was fine though he felt I should eat more fruit and vegetables.

Then a few weeks later the CAT scan - there I've remembered it - Google is my fweng.

An hour lying in a tube, ears blocked to lessen the incredible noise as the grinding, whirring, shouting, screaming X Rays pushed back and forth, side to side… "You can have music and headphones", they yelled. "Only if they are my own hits" I bellowed back.

Some days waiting then the expert summoned me in.

"I have very good news", he said. "In all my years I have never seen someone of 80 with the brain of a 40 year old. Everybody over 50 has little mini strokes, often whilst they are asleep and don't notice but which always leave tiny scars on the surface of the brain. Yours is the only one I've ever seen of your age without a single blemish. More than that, everybody's brain shrinks as they grow older. Yours hasn't done so - not by a centimetre".

"So I don't have Alzheimers?".

"No, not even a hint of it".

"So why do I keep forgetting things?".

80
That's All Folks!

"That's just age. Your brain has got so much in it there's no room for anything new. The computer needs a reboot. Unfortunately we haven't yet come up with a way to do that to a brain".

He saw I was disappointed and asked why.

"Well, if I have to appear in court again, on either criminal historical charges or civil ones, it would be impossible to defend myself".

He looked shocked so I explained my situation and he became quite angry.

"You would not believe how many elderly patients I get now, requesting a survey because they are facing similar charges. Literally hundreds of old people. Sometimes they are, indeed, going senile but more often the stress and strain of the claims and the investigation is driving them around the bend. I have no idea whether they are guilty or innocent but there is an epidemic of this kind of persecution".

"And the effect it has on their loved ones, particularly the older ones, is equally frightening. I'd be happy, if you need it, to do a letter explaining that, in my opinion, anybody over 70 would be unable to defend themselves against claims going back 30 or 40 years".

"30 or 40? And then some", I replied, "try 1970!".

For those of you mathematically challenged or even suffering from early onset senility, that's 55 years.

JONATHAN KING

I remember one of my favourite writers, Iris Murdoch, became senile and continued writing but sadly it showed in her work. My mum, mentioned beforehand, had a fear of it, having nursed my uncle Sir Kenneth Lee - after whom I was named - through it. Alzheimers or not, I've found, penning this tome (penning, you notice, another P word) I have to keep referring to 65 My Life So Far and 70 FFFY and even GUILTY to make sure I'm not repeating myself and boring you to death, gentle reader. Those works are constantly thumbed as I type. Break now - just let me check.

Actually this chapter has been easy as the events have all taken place since the publication of the other volumes. But otherwise I can hear my trusty loyal assistant James going "NO! Not that bloody John Lennon story again!" And forcing me to take it out.

It's not easy having a good time - even smiling makes my face ache - a quote from my dear friend Richard O'Brien's Rocky Horror Show. I had breakfast with Richard recently and he revealed he'd only made around a million quid from that classic masterwork - he was ripped off - weren't we all - by Michael "Chalky" White. Who had given me 20% of all profits to the project, in return for my huge investment, and then, when the show caught on, quietly bankrupted the company which had signed my contract after transferring the rights to another

80
That's All Folks!

of his companies. Perfectly legal I gather.

So you see there has been a point to this health update. It's not just a fat old queen rambling on. It reflects on the state of humanity, on society which not only fails to take into account the problems of ageing, and much more in this brave new world, but doesn't care.

Now I know that's a silly thing to say. Why should "society" care? It's not a person. It's an organisation - cold, efficient, dedicated to doing the best for the members. Which, in many cases, means giving readers, viewers and listeners A GREAT STORY. By exaggerating and inflating it, "the worst case I've ever seen in my career as a top cop" (see my portrayal in Vile Pervert The Musical). Without considering the repercussions.

Not just on innocent people. On perpetrators too. And on their families. Surely even a mass murderer is a human being and should be treated with kindness. Yes, they should be punished. Yes, they should be kept away from the rest of us as long as they remain a danger. But look after them. Respect them. Be kind to them. And also - how about their relations and friends? Do they deserve to be punished?

My Mum - see above - was incredibly touched by the almost universally positive and supportive reaction to my very public arrest, trial and conviction in 2001. Having lived in the area for most of the 56 years of my life, she knew almost everyone and said, to a man and woman, she only received sympathy and support from everybody. Whether or not they believed in my innocence or considered me guilty, they had only kindness to offer to her and my family.

Sir Brian Leveson, in front of whom I appeared for some hours during his interviews for The Leveson Report on media, has just published another report on the legal system. He makes the valid point that since times have changed and do so regularly, the system should adapt with it. I agree - and not only in law - in everything humanity has failed to change the structures of society as things like The Internet have taken hold.

One of the many, hugely positive aspects of what happened to me in 2001 was the experience of spending three and a half years in prison and being able to see what the system does to people. I've mentioned elsewhere that I was horrified to find that at least 50% of inmates could neither read nor write, and my letters on their behalf to wives, children, parents and others brought incredible joy to them and their loved ones. I was frequently embraced, hugged and kissed by total strangers in the Visitors Room, so much so that officers stopped trying to tell them NOT to do it - it became a fact of life that I was to receive gratitude from those who, at last, had genuine communication with the prisoners.

80
That's All Folks!

A couple of detours here - one day, in HMP Maidstone, about 50 of us inmates were walking to work in the print shop. A new officer with an enormous German Shepherd dog was on the far side of the square. The dog pulled his lead from his holder and shot towards us. The inmates scattered in terror like chickens. The dog leapt up at me, put his paws on my shoulders and licked my face.
When the breathless, panting officer arrived he apologised profusely. "I'm sorry JK, he remembered you from Belmarsh". Indeed, during my six months in Belmarsh Prison I has befriended all the dogs there, adoring them, especially Alsatians. In fact, on my first day, drugs searchers had arrived in my cell with their dog - a cocker spaniel. We had instantly fallen in love and his officer brought him to me daily, officially to search for drugs but in fact for a cuddle and a scratch.

I became quite popular with those working in the prisons I went to, as I contributed to their lives with advice and friendship and ideas. One particular prisoner was ignored by everyone, due to his heinous crimes - I never asked what they were - and an officer said to me "you really shouldn't speak to him JK - we have to report all contacts and it could reflect badly on you in the future". I replied "when I came into this I vowed that if anyone wanted to speak to me I would let them, and I don't intend to break that promise".

That odd character once burst into tears in my cell ("you're going to laugh at me JK but I hate it when the yolk of an egg gets broken and they know that, so break my yolks every time"). I had a quiet word with the inmates serving food and asked them to stop doing it. "But he's so awful JK". "Yes, he is but why make his life even worse? Stop doing it, as a favour to me".

Almost every inmate owed me favours for advice or kindness I'd shown them. So they stopped breaking his yolks.

Days later he was almost uncontrollable in his gratitude. Not because his yolks were no longer being broken but because someone, another human being, had listened to him and taken him seriously. It wasn't so much that I'd done something, but that I'd listened to him.

As a result I'll bet you, when released, he never offended again. He'll have led a blameless life - as a favour to me.

One officer had a teenage son who was desperate to get into the junior team of the local football club. He asked for my advice. I gave it to him. His son got into the team and the officer said his son was really grateful and would like to come in and thank me in person.

"You're joking", I said. "You are aware what I'm in here for?".

80
That's All Folks!

"Yes, but we all know you're innocent".

"Thank you - but that's not the way the media works", I replied.

I had a great time in prison, mainly helping others. Not a single problem except once when two young new inmates hissed "Nonce" at me. I took them into their cell.

"I have to tell you that next Sunday both your names and photos - and the reasons you're both in here - are on the Front Page of the News of the World, exposing the fact that you're my lovers in here".

They went white.

"No", I said. "But it could be, if I decided to leak the story - easily done from here. So I suggest a little respect, please".

From then on they grovelled with polite behaviour.

Most prisoners, innocent or guilty, were far more morally upright than the media people I'd mixed with before my (wrongful) conviction.

Chapter 16

JOHNNY REGGAE, ROD STEWART AND THE SKINHEADS

I've always loved the sunshine and, finding very little of it in London in the summer, I've tended to go abroad for a couple of months, July and August.

In the winter I used to leave for Morocco or Tunisia on Boxing Day, after celebrating Christmas with my mother and family at Cobbetts, but after she died in 2007, by which time my nephews were grown up and not into things like Christmas, ditto my godchildren, I took to going away for the winter before my birthday, so I could spend both December and January swimming in the sun.

My swimming was not just for pleasure. I felt it was a health necessity, five hours a day, simply doing breast stroke, thinking and planning as I swam, following it by writing, eating, drinking and sleeping. And soon my summers extended too - May, June, July and August, with a couple of trips back to England in the middle for work

80
That's All Folks!

reasons, leaving the car abroad in a secure place.

For winter, the nearest place to reach was Morocco and only Marrakech was, and is, south enough to guarantee swimming weather. When younger I was happy to fly to distant lands and often wintered in Hawaii or Australia or the Far East, but I went off the long flights. After my beloved Concorde ended, I tried to fly as little as possible. I sometimes drove leisurely down through France and Spain, via favourite cities like Paris and Seville - in Europe in the summer it became mainly France and Italy, with Rome an essential regular and sometimes taking in Munich, my favourite city in Germany.

Since 1971 I've called my breaks "the Johnny Reggae trips" as that one single brought me in so much money - I wrote it, published it and produced it, even sang on it in the choruses in falsetto, put it out under the name The Piglets, no artiste payments, all session work, and it sold millions around the globe, reaching No2 in the UK.

The reason I called them The Piglets was because the little skinhead girls at the time looked like little piglets as they danced around their handbags in the clubs, the biggest at the time being The Walton Hop - more about that, run and owned by my dear friend Deniz Corday, in GUILTY.

Not a lot has been written about girl skinheads, as they clearly didn't actually shave their heads, but there were millions of them and it was one of them, at the Hop, who introduced me to her boyfriend as Johnny Reggae, her nickname for him because he loved Reggae music. I asked if he would mind if I wrote a song called that and he granted me permission.

When the record took off, exploding days after sale, thanks, originally, to the DJ John Peel, who loved it, I got a call from my friend Derek Chinnery, at the time Controller of Radio One at the BBC.

"Jonathan I'm hearing rumours that there are sexual innuendos in the lyric", he said, "like He's Always On The Bone" - a slang word for an erection at the time was a BONER.

"No, no, Derek, it's always on the PHONE".

"And I'm His, Here, Inside is apparently getting obscene gestures on the dance floor".

"I can't help what they do - it's in her heart, of course".

"And worst of all - He Looks Me In The Eye When He Shoots".

"It's a football reference, Derek, for when he scores a goal and she's in the stands".

"OK, I'll believe you".

A few weeks later I noticed that the track was getting so much airplay that it was affecting sales - people tired of it quickly and didn't need to hear it so much on the radio; I wanted them to go out and buy it, as I was making

80
That's All Folks!

£1 a copy and it did sell millions in the end. So I called him up and said "Derek, I'm sorry; I must admit I lied to you; it's full of sexual innuendoes".

"Jonathan, I am not accepting this call" and he put the phone down.

The lady who sang or spoke the lead arrived at my door with her young baby clutched in her arms, exposed to the elements, wailing and crying. "Can't I have a royalty?", she squealed. "Barbara, like all session singers I've paid you a fortune in the past singing on flops that have lost me money - it's your job." The union backed me, as, indeed, they should have done. Session work was and is hugely rewarding and session musicians can always request, before a session, a royalty instead of a fee but very few do.

Producing is a gamble and a very expensive one. I was lucky in that, for a short time my investments paid off. Those ten to twenty years funded my life and career for most of my 80 years. I'm still living off the pension from those times when I was the Producer of the Year.

Artistes forget the importance of others. Stars frequently believe their own image and think they were 99% responsible for their success when, in reality, they contribute 5% at most. It's the writers of the songs, producers, engineers and arrangers - plus session musicians as many groups cannot play. Then, enamoured by celebrity, they morph into "stars".

Some actually retain human qualities. I first met Rod Stewart when he was a grave digger, wanting to be a singer. He did have a great voice - Python Lee Jackson was, I remember, an early example. I've mentioned John Peel - a huge supporter of The Faces and Rod - he once appeared on Top of the Pops as a member of Rod's band, pretending to play a banjo or ukulele on one of his hits.

I remember, when I took over The Brits trying to save them after the Sam Fox/Mick Fleetwood disaster year, I asked Rod if he'd appear. He readily agreed and suggested we keep it secret - a terrific idea which brought the house down - he was a big star then.

He arrived with our mutual friend Michael Summerton. I bumped into Rod recently in Morocco and we had a long nostalgia session about Michael.

Anyway, when, after his performance, they left, Rod sneered at Michael who had collected his "goody bag" before leaving. Believe it or not, nobody in the UK had copied the US idea of giving goody bags to artistes and their friends as a thank you after they showed up at the events like the Oscars or Grammys. Michael started going through the contents. Fantastic aftershaves and perfumes, watches, all kinds of top of the range goodies I'd blagged from luxury manufacturers in order to boost their images.

Rod gasped - and made the driver reverse, go back to

80
That's All Folks!

the venue, and came rushing backstage to collect his bag, which he'd refused when originally offered it. I reminded Rod of this and several other incidents as we lay by the pool in Rabat. His wife - a lovely and very nice lady - was highly amused when I pointed out that Rod and I had had dinner 8 times in our lives and I had paid for every one (Scottish). He said "Right - I'll pay tonight". "Why break the habit of a lifetime", I answered. Yes - I paid - for the ninth time.

Anyway, back to the 1960s... I remember once driving down to Brighton, I used to go there a lot for weekends, staying at the Grand, on the road down through Brixton I spotted a skinhead sitting on a wall, dangling his heavy Doc Martin boots. Two things attracted me. One - he had long hair, unusual for a skinhead. And Two - he was absolutely gorgeous.

We chatted, exchanged phone numbers and got together.

He was the most popular boy in Brixton and I made it very clear what my scene was, but he just wasn't interested. I got more and more friendly with him and his "gang", a group of skinhead supporters of Chelsea club, known at the time as The Shed, essentially hooligans and monsters but in reality 16 or 17 year olds, full of energy and fun and rather similar to the lads in Rome, the San Basilio district where my friend Nino Mulas lived and full of villains, where, if they liked you and took you to their hearts, they would never abuse the friendship and would protect you at all times. They didn't care about sexuality - remember the Krays?. They liked or disliked the person.

They were all very attractive, in that strange teenage way, and most were quite happy to experiment sexually with me. Only one lad, who I think was gay, asked me please not to tell his friends, which I never did. The rest were absolutely fine and were well aware that I adored the original boy, who they all tried to persuade to go with me but who smilingly, gently refused.

Then one day he decided he wanted to experiment. We spent a wonderful night together after which he said it had been fabulous but he didn't think he'd ever do it again. "I'm not bisexual; I'm King sexual", he said, "I love you but my future is with the ladies".

I wrote a song for him called I Just Wanna Say Thank You.

A few years later the gang got into terrible trouble at a riot where a police officer was blinded. Though this was before the era of Joint Enterprise, a dozen or so, including all my friends, were charged. I organised the top lawyer in London at the time, a horrid gay man called David Jonas who represented many queens in difficulty with the law, to look after my boy.

I got a phone call later from his grateful parents - he'd

80
That's All Folks!

escaped with a smack on the wrist. All the others went to jail or borstal, as it was then, and the one who was responsible for blinding the officer, who I did not know, spent many years inside.

Which actually didn't do my boy any favours, as all those in Brixton thought he'd bought himself freedom, through his contacts, whilst their friends were doing time. We lost touch but I always have fond memories of him. Someone who really knew his own mind and was happy to conform to some stereotypes but not others.

Every time I hear about East End gangsters like the aforementioned Krays I think of the strange gay undercurrent running through that strata of working class families. Far more sensible than many others - less influenced by the mores of society or religion and more interested in genuine, harmless experiences. Of course, for females there was the danger of pregnancy and all that entailed but for males even health issues were easily solved.

Remember this was the time of antibiotics curing almost any sexually transmitted disease. But also remember this was the time when gay relationships were crimes and many of the working classes saw it as yet another silly regulation, to be broken wherever possible.

We celebrities had a pet "clap doctor" who saw us privately and gave us the antibiotics needed, avoiding any publicity that might have come from being seen in the public "clap clinic".

I often wonder what male teenagers today do, when faced by stimulation from another male. If the other is younger, it's seen as paedophilia, even if both are under 16. Almost all religions condemn it as a sin. Despite the gay world now being accepted by society legally, in most countries, the reality is far from that. Romances like Romeo and Juliet are considered, by many, to be disgraceful, I'm sure, just as "You're Gay" was the playground insult of my youth, "Paedo!" is the word hurled at the prettier and more popular children today. Every time I see a death of a teenager, often "unexplained", I think of that - adults cannot escape assisting the spread of bigotry and hatred and children being cruel, often through jealousy.

I remember I avoided such smears at school and University by having sex with the potential bullies. As a result, terrified of being found out, they never picked on me.

The other aspect of teenage sexually connected deaths that disturbs me is so often, I'm absolutely certain, those deaths were the result of sexual experimentation such as masturbating whilst hanging oneself - something I've never been tempted to do but people, even the very young, are all very different. There is even a term for it.

80
That's All Folks!

Auto-erotic Asphyxia or, as I gather the kids call it, scarfing, because they tend to use their scarves.

I still have my old Charterhouse scarf, rescued when we cleaned out our mother's house, Cobbetts, after her death in 2007, hidden away in my old room at the top of the stairs, moth balled and safe, pink and blue stripes. I can't imagine anything less sexually arousing than dangling from it whilst fiddling with my flaccid organ, but each to their own.

Parents coming home to find their son dead, hanging, in what was clearly a state of arousal, never seem to want to admit this. Even to themselves. They go on about the causes of suicide, mount campaigns, start charities. Whilst, all the time, looking the wrong way. As a species, certainly in the West, we still seem shocked and horrified by sex whereas it is an incredibly harmless way of getting enjoyment and even giving enjoyment to others. My personal pleasure.

It's one of the major problems of humanity; this twisted attitude to sexuality. It poisons religion. It kills children. It's there for practical reasons - of races promulgating and not losing population but God knows why it's still around. Actually he or she doesn't know - I've discussed it with them and they are as confused as I am. Other species have no hangups about sex. Why do humans?

To return briefly to dear Derek Chinnery. We had started on the wrong foot in 1965, when he was producing the Pete Murray show, and I turned up as a guest with two friends I was due to take to dinner - Kenny Everett and Dave Cash.

Pete recognised them immediately and insisted on them coming on air too. Derek, knowing they were technically criminals, pirates on Radio London Big L and not to be sanctioned by the BBC at any level, gently refused.

They had a huge argument and Derek won. I did the interview alone. But he didn't forgive me for months for putting him in that position.

Later, however, we got to be close friends. After he retired, in this century, I asked if I could visit him up in Geordie Land Newcastle and take him to dinner. He was delighted - he showed me proudly around his little bungalow that he'd spent ages "doing up" - we sat and had drinks in his garden, then he came back to my hotel for a delicious dinner, during which we gossiped at length about old times - particularly his wife Doreen, who I'd loved. She had died some time back.

Doreen and I would get together at functions and have a lovely quiet giggle ("Have you seen Blackburn's hair???") about things she couldn't really giggle with Derek about as he was the Boss.

80
That's All Folks!

It took me forever driving up there, but I don't think I've ever felt more satisfied. It really made Derek's year, as he told me many times. People in retirement tend to get forgotten.

Remember by then I was a Vile Pervert, not to be associated with. And the whole Savile thing had exploded, which Derek found distressing. He had seen nothing sexually dodgy about Savile, probably because there was nothing to see - until the media decided there was, after his death. Retired Chinnery was hounded by the tabloids. But friendship is far more important than media. And talking of Pete Murray who is now not only 99 years old but, as I type, on Boom Radio. A superb DJ, to this day.

The big FOUR in the early 60s, before the pirates really took over were Pete, Alan "Fluff" Freeman, a lovely, cuddly supportive man who was brilliant at re-inventing himself into different genres of music, Jimmy Savile, who really didn't care about the music but had been shrewd enough to realise he could get celebrity and fame and a lot of money, almost ALL spent on charity, from being a DJ, and David Jacobs.

David was a real gentleman - I'm sure he always presented his radio shows in a dinner jacket and tie, very much "old school" but younger than most of his contemporaries - handsome, erudite and polite.

The four of them were brilliant contrasts - moving the

BBC into the new generation where most DJs were in their twenties and far "groovier".

We kids in 1965 respected them all in their different ways. And others like Jimmy Young, who had been a very successful "pop" star in the era when they were "crooners", and Terry Wogan, who took longer to emerge but was essentially a younger member of that older cast.

I remember getting a phone call from David Jacobs, it must have been in 1966 or 1967, asking me if we could have lunch. It turned out that his son Jeremy was about to go to Charterhouse School and was very nervous - would I take him for lunch and reassure him. Which I did. No - nothing more - for a start he was too young. Remember my rule - over 16 only. But also my morality ("JK is the most moral person I've ever met but only to his own morality" Clive Selwood) forbade even a hint or suggestion under such situations. I was speaking to him as a friend's son. Taboo.

Jeremy died very young; in a car accident I believe. I was also friends with David's daughter Joanna who occasionally, internet being what it is, gets in touch to say hello.

Whilst we've progressed, on the surface, old bigotry remains strong, like the feet of a swan paddling away. I remember when I was first arrested in 2000 and even again in 2015, I got very little support from the gay

80
That's All Folks!

community, despite having been a leader of the protest movement with songs from the 1960s like Gay Girl and I Don't Wanna Be Gay.

Understandable. Having gotten freedom and acceptance, the last thing the gay world wants to do is to be seen to be supportive of paedophiles.

DOH!

Chapter 17

THE CCRC, POLICE & CRIME COMMISSIONERS AND VICTIMS

The events of 2015 onwards were covered in detail in both the book and film GUILTY and the booklet Not A Knee On The Neck, which, as I've mentioned, so infuriated one of the Surrey Cops that she complained to her Union who insisted I withdraw it from further paper publication. It remains available as an E-Book.

She was right of course. I named her, for all the ghastly mistakes she and other Surrey officers had made. And the Surrey PCC at the time, David Munro. Police and Executives feel they have a right NOT to be mentioned in the media. Just as they never expect to be punished for making mistakes.

In fact, after PCC Munro had been no help at all in correcting the mistakes made by the Surrey force, including three Deaths In Custody that they had failed to report to the (then) IPCC, I campaigned in Surrey during the subsequent election for a new PCC, giving away

80
That's All Folks!

copies of the book. Dozens of people said they weren't even aware that there was a PCC election and said they would now definitely vote - for someone else. Munro, a dreadful old queen, stood for re-election and was soundly beaten.

But it's worth examining some aspects of this debacle in here, since neither 65 nor 70 contained any info as they all covered the periods before my 2015 arrest. And it is topically appropriate, in 2025, as the new interim Head of the CCRC has just been appointed. **DAME Vera Baird**.

There are three things against Vera Baird. First, she was, or has been, a PCC - Police and Crime Commissioner. My experience with such creatures has not been good. They tend to support the Chief Constable, no matter what.

Secondly, she's been a Victims Commissioner. Such people tend to support and believe "victims", whether true or false. And not see any "victims" who don't conform to the accepted media stereotype. For the simplistic, "victims" tend to be female, innocent, abused and incredibly brave to do something about it - like fight back.

Thirdly, she's a woman. The females of the species tend to stick together and the majority of "victims" are women. They find it hard or impossible to believe that women could lie or exaggerate. They find it easy to see men as stronger and less feminine. Indeed, many are.

But let's give her time and, for the moment, believe the best - that she will improve the CCRC, especially the women looking at MY wrongful conviction from 25 years ago... so, so long ago.

As HHJ Paget said, summing up at my 2001 trial, "I accept it was all so long ago and the defendant has no hope of saying "I was in America at the time" or similar". Except I could and did and was and would have found out, during the trial, had I been given a few minutes to prepare a defence for the new, changed dates.

Which I wasn't. Standard judicial behaviour as my defence Junior, William McCormick, told me as we accepted the Judges' decision.

Anyway, in 2018 I approached the appalling Munro and told him the appalling Ephgrave, then Chief Constable of Surrey and the only police person the PCC has any power over, should fire the appalling Hayes and Bridge for not reporting three Deaths In Custody to the Independent Police Watchdog, then IPCC now IOPC. As was strictly dictated by police law.

My friends Rob Randall and Deniz Corday had also been arrested and questioned. Rob killed himself; Deniz died through stress. The third man, Lawrence, was wrongly accused and questioned about being a victim of

80
That's All Folks!

Deniz' and then grilled about me. A quadriplegic, the stress killed him too.

"It was the worst thing that ever happened to me", he said when we visited him. "How about your motor cycle crash?". "No, this was far worse because it was destroying my closest friend and I couldn't do anything about it. Plus I was younger then and able to cope. You don't know what it's like being in a wheel chair. Oh, they were perfectly nice and polite. They asked if I minded if they searched - "looked around" - my flat - they had no search warrant, of course. I said no, fine - I have nothing to hide. I could hear them going through cupboards and drawers as they tried to convince me to say Deniz abused me. When I refused, they started on you. Had you ever made any jokes? Asked questions in bad taste? After they left it took ages to put everything back. They took a few items - with my permission, naturally; a leather jacket Deniz had given me. But you don't realise how exhausting it is to put the bread back two shelves lower so you can reach it and other similar things. Being quadriplegic requires so many small details, built up over years of training. It took me hours. They treated me, politely, but as if I was a criminal. Next day I was rushed to hospital. I've only just come out and I still can't keep food down".

There was a half empty plate of food in front of him.

Two days later he died. Aged 56 - the age I was when I was arrested in 2001.

He had been in Stoke Mandeville hospital after his crash, aged 20. Jimmy Savile often visited - "a pain in the arse. Always trying to cheer us up. But most of us never wanted to be cheered up".

"Did he ever try anything on with you?".

"God no; there would have been a riot".

The other "victim" Surrey Police tried to set up against Deniz was Liam, a friend's grandson, whom Deniz had virtually brought up, as his Dad had left them at birth. Liam however, fit and young, had simply told Surrey Police to fuck off and slammed the door in their face.

All three murdered victims of Surrey Police were Surrey Residents. Read about them in greater detail in GUILTY and in Not A Knee On The Neck.

It is a very strict rule, in the police Code of Behaviour, that such deaths must be reported to the watchdog and fully investigated. Ephgrave refused to do so. Munro accepted his excuses.

Ephgrave left Surrey Police for a job with the MET and rose steadily up the slippery ranks, as they tend to do, eventually even applying to be Met Chief and beaten by Mark Rowley who, as it happened, had been CC of Surrey back in 2001. He currently heads up the Serious Fraud Office, appropriately.

80
That's All Folks!

Munro seems to have retired from public life. Although he may still be scrabbling along as a local minor Surrey councillor. But my guess is that, at a Surrey dinner when he was PCC, he may have sat near Alison Rose, then boss of RBS. She may have told him I had banked with NatWest for 60 years. He may have asked her to drop me.

For whatever reason, in 2019 NatWest dumped me, just as they did Nigel Farage some years later, after, I believe, an indiscreet dinner attended by Alison Rose. When cares? I'm now with several much better banks and would urge anyone never to go anywhere near one of the RBS banks under any circumstances. And certainly never have anything to do with the ghastly Alison Rose by any other name.

There's not a lot to be said for Police and Crime Commissioners, a stupid idea started by Theresa May, one of the few Prime Ministers and Home Secretaries to have been even worse than Liz Truss.

And I'm sure Vera Baird, when she was a PCC, did not allow police to get away with murder, as David Munro and Nick Ephgrave did. One thing I'm certain about - if both had reined in the rogue officers who failed to report the killings to the IPCC, neither Sarah Everard nor David Carrick's rape victims would have suffered. The top cops, nervous about the scandal potential, would have cleaned out the stables. No more using a warrant card to rape and murder an innocent young girl.

Wayne Couzens was a direct result of police incompetence and "protecting their own". "Stand by your (man) fellow officers" has been a cop rule for years - rather like Keir Starmer as DPP's "you will be believed even if you are lying". Yes - the "lying" bit was only implied, not stated, but the meaning is the same. And Baird's job as Interim Boss of the CCRC, gives her the opportunity, if she wants, to throw a hand grenade into the system.

The CPS should not be allowed to change the dates on an indictment without giving the defendant a single second to investigate potential alibis.

Bad law. Bad Judges.

Police should NOT be allowed to hold back vital evidence that a "victim" is lying until after a trial. If I were a Juror on the JK 2001 trial and now found, reading this, that I'd been fooled into believing that something happened that clearly never did, I'd feel betrayed. By bent cops and the system.

I was terribly rude about HHJ Taylor- calling her the bumblebee in GUILTY until she turned out to be an angel. Saw the lies, realised the truth and not only insisted I was acquitted in 2018 but refused the CPS request for any retrials. God bless her - I wish there were more

80
That's All Folks!

Judges like her.

So I give Baird the benefit of the doubt. She has until just after my birthday in early December 2026 to sort out the CCRC. If my high profile case goes back to the Court of Appeal and it throws my wrongful conviction from 2001 out, it will have enormous ramifications. Yes; it should have happened years ago. Yes: I have every right to sue Surrey Police for the £50million I lost as Global Chairman of EMI and nobody can ever repair the damage done to the music industry by my removal from it.

But most important YES; the hundreds of wrongly convicted men and women sitting in jails across the country must then have THEIR convictions at least considered.

I quote from Dame Vera… *"It is vital the public can have confidence in an organisation whose constitutional importance is so central to a fair and just system."*

It is indeed vital and if Dame Vera truly understands that, she should be brilliant in the job. But I seem to remember, in past roles, she supported criminals trying to make cash from false allegations from having to reveal phone messages or texts that showed they were lying.

Falling for the simplistic argument that "victims" should not have their phones, iPads or laptops examined. In case there was evidence they were lying. Of course they should be seized and examined. Of course they should not automatically be believed. A balanced investigation should take no sides.

And anyone who feels they should not be allowed to look at all evidence from every angle needs their head examined. By concealing evidence, they are colluding in crimes.

It is easy, these days, for the vast majority to believe the simple caricatures. "Women never lie". Really? "Children always tell the truth". Oh yes?

Hopefully Dame Vera is as aware as any intelligent person that there are layers of truth and reasons for people to exaggerate or lie or adapt stories for their benefit. Many speak the truth. Many others lie. Men and women. And most are somewhere in between, when they are persuaded or cajoled to make money for lawyers or get praise and promotion for police - much with legitimate intent but a substantial amount twisted, to get results.

The head of the CCRC needs to be independent and balanced, to search for the truth and to try to get their staff to work hard to find and refer such miscarriages of justice to the Courts.

Money should be no object, and I think the CCRC should have a huge increase in budget within weeks. They should employ the very best. They must use the freelance skills and abilities of people like the late Bob Woffinden,

80
That's All Folks!

Ludovic Kennedy and others. They must not be afraid to irritate and annoy Judges who have got it wrong. The system is shattered - it is NOT "fair and just". We are currently overwhelmed by theories about Lucy Letby, a nurse convicted of murdering babies whose trial was clearly unfair. I have no idea whether she is innocent, guilty or somewhere in between. But I am certain the system is broken and her trial was a farce.

I've mentioned before the very good three Judges in the Malkinson appeal. It would have been easy enough simply to quash his conviction on new DNA grounds. But they decided they would look at his other reasons for appeal and found that two of the four other grounds SHOULD have been referred back to the Court of Appeal years earlier and they WOULD have had his conviction overturned.

That was the devastating decision that opened the door to other past CCRC decisions - including those made in my case.

It's easier and simpler for media to ignore this. It's better for the politicians and the judiciary to say these situations are "vanishingly rare". They are not. They are the majority because most convicted are simply not bright enough and not wealthy enough to know what they need to do.

I relied on my expensive lawyers costing one million

pounds in 2001. Do not hire a dog and bark yourself. They were awful. They looked good, sounded good but let me down appallingly. I relied on the judiciary to correct their mistakes, to put them right if they wanted truth. They didn't.

Most people cannot survive a wrong decision by a jury, a spell in prison, all the ramifications. I did survive and, as I say elsewhere, my brilliant Private Investigator, William Merritt said it was my specific instructions to him that enabled him to find so much evidence that got me acquitted and HHJ Taylor to refuse any retrials - a very rare judicial act.

I don't blame lawyers or others. It's a full time job for police and the CPS. Only we, the accused, know the specifics required. Only we have the time and the inclination to read every word, study every line, spot the lies, the contradictions, the mistakes and the errors. Which, in the end, show dishonesty, deliberate or otherwise, and reveal the fundamental flaws in so many fake claims.

Over to you, Vera.

A recent scandal in Surrey concerns a man called Stephen Ireland. He was one of the main movers and shakers of the PRIDE movement in the area and was a close favourite of then PCC Munro as well as the two Chief Constables Nick Ephgrave and Gavin Stephens.

80
That's All Folks!

Munro supported Ireland whilst choosing to ignore my complaints about Surrey Police, met with him numerous times and backed him again and again.

In June 2025 Ireland was sentenced to 24 years in prison for raping a 12 year old boy.

I don't know anything about Munro's association with Ireland and his friends but clearly the then Surrey PCC was not a good judge of character.

But this case, or what we can read about it in the media, shows further lunacy.

It appears the boy was very mature for his age, knew or had decided he was gay and not only consented to the relationship but started it.

OK - nobody should take advantage of a child and the practical risks and legal situation should have made it clear that nothing sexual should happen until after he turned 16.

But 24 years in prison? Murderers get less.

It may be there were factors not reported by media that influenced the Judge. But I suspect the reaction from the media influenced the length of the sentence. Indeed, I suspect it will be greatly reduced on appeal.

Google the man and decide for yourself. There are hundreds of similar cases, most, like this, hardly reported, certainly not on a national level.

Food for thought. Assuming, gentle reader, you are capable of depth of thought. So few are, these days.

Chapter 18

FOR THOSE ABOUT TO DIE - WE SALUTE YOU!

Those reading previous volumes of my autobiography will know all about Max Clifford, portrayed by me in a Max wig, as Waxie Maxie, in my film Vile Pervert The Musical. Max described that as "remarkably accurate".

Past readers will know how he started my downfall, probably for a soon-to-be-fired EMI executive or his wife, because I'd agreed, in 2000, to become Global Chairman of EMI at the, then, hefty salary of £5million a year with a firm ten year contract. Max was a PR person, specialising in selling stories to the tabloids about footballers and women who claimed to have been assaulted by them.

Karma kicked in. When we left him, in 70 FFFY, he was languishing in a prison cell for many years - far longer than me, as his sentences were consecutive as opposed to mine which were concurrent. For abusing under age females. Read all about it.

80
That's All Folks!

Since then, he's dead.

In prison, without his beloved cigars. Not, as far as I know, from any prison violence but simply because Lady Karma moved in and wiped him out.

It's the way things go. Other characters from Volumes One and Two have prospered and developed but many have fallen off the twig. I'm still here aged 80. God knows for how much longer. I'd like to reach 90 or even 100; to retain all my marbles and not to fall apart physically. Mainly because there is so much more to do. As our species seems to go more and more bonkers, one man, me, would like to point it in a better direction. Especially if, as some suspect, we return in different guises.

I'm not sure how I'll cope if I come back as a human. God forbid, I could be female and I cannot stand the ideas of bleeding every month or, even worse, spending months getting more and more bloated until I have to suffer incredible pain before producing ghastly little brats. No, please.

Or I may come back as a fish. Or a bird. Or a tree. Or a butterfly. A friend used to call me The Butterfly That Stamped. I rather liked that description.

Remember I became Internet savvy way back in the 1980s, forced to use online for my column in The Sun.

I've revealed in 70 FFFY the rise and fall of the Sons of Admirals group. Back in the first decade of this century, I felt the time was right for a boy band and had made contact with several suitable teenage candidates including Tom Milsom (Hexachordal), Charlie McDonnell (CharlieIsSoCoolLike) and Alex Day (Nerimon).

In the first decade of the new century, all had started on the fresh new internet Social Media front and had gained big followings.

"I think you could all be huge", I said.

"Yes, please", they answered. The tale of our success is in 70 FFFY. But I left out certain crucial parts back then and updates are required, now they are all in their thirties, middle aged men. And other artistes from that era have appeared and disappeared.

Their manager was going to be Richard Griffiths, a friend from the previous century who had started a management company, Modest. after losing his job at the top of BMG, which I had helped him obtain. One of his contacts from the record label days was my old friend Simon Cowell and, when Sons of Admirals fell apart, Simon, spotting the gap in the market, created One Direction, to be managed, like most of his other X Factor/BGT acts, by Modest.

The reason Sons of Admirals fell apart was simple - me.

I'd watched them being interviewed on some

80
That's All Folks!

children's TV show after the first release, an excellent version of Cat Stevens' Here Comes My Baby, brilliantly produced by Tommy, with a great video by Charlie, charted. I'd suggested the song, which I knew from my 1960s friendship with Cat Stevens. It had also been a hit for The Tremeloes.

I summoned the lads to a lunch.

"OK", I said, "the band now splits up".

"Why? It's going great".

"Because I've never seen anything so awful as Charlie during that TV interview. He clearly hated being there. He doesn't want to be famous. He's only going along with it because we're all friends. It is child abuse. Right Charlie?"

He blushed and nodded. That was the end of the group. And, as we all now know, One Direction took over. I believe it is the responsibility of those behind big acts to be sure each member is staying "on the rails". OK I had no professional interest in Sons of Admirals, and only did what I did as a friend, offering advice and suggestions - all the more valuable as none of it would affect my life or be provoked by my bank balance.

I was able, not influenced by greed for cash, to see that, had Sons of Admirals continued, Charlie would probably, by now, be dead.

It's always been that way - even in professional

situations. That was why I gave Genesis to Tony Stratton Smith without demanding any over-ride or royalty. That was why I advised Sam Fox how to become a pop star, without ever making a penny from her.

Alex and I remained friends - still are; he's agreed to edit this book for me. He went on to great solo success, making a fortune; then left music and is now very successful in IT with a beautiful long term girlfriend who is also a friend of mine. He had a nasty brush with the False Allegations Industry but escaped unscathed. And was able to give me terrific ammunition when, in 2015, Surrey Police tried and failed again to stitch me up. More later.

Tommy, likewise, had an encounter with false allegations and likewise survived. It is almost inevitable these days - success breeds liars after money or revenge or even just being noticed. That's what social media is all about.

I remember, in the early days, Alex asked me if I felt the three of them, he, Charlie and Tommy, were like a modern day equivalent of the Romantic Poets - Shelley; Keats; Byron. I said NO, they would make the mistakes that others would learn from, and that was exactly what happened.

Tommy went, musically, his own way - very experimental. Into a very different art form.

80
That's All Folks!

And Charlie left the country. Did reasonably well but seems to have had a disturbed undercurrent of concern which, sadly, he never chose to discuss with me. He has now embraced his feminine side, calls himself SHE and is a member of the trans gender community. Charlie was a nice kid but, I always felt, boring. I suspect I was wrong in that, and he just kept his self knowledge buried deep inside him, shown to nobody. Alex shared a house with him for years and never suspected the truth as we now know it, almost 20 years later.

I wonder whether the fact that I'm now 80 has affected my ability to hear and break hits. Or whether the changing face of the music industry has meant that today's "hits" are no longer mass appeal, cross over hits but simply appeal to that section of music lovers who are attracted to a specific sound or artiste. I've listened to dozens of Taylor Swift songs and have yet to find one that would appeal to anybody not a Swiftie,

Or is it that the new world requires different ways of breaking hits? Social media has changed everything. The days of radio and TV are long gone - except for the masters of the new art, like Simon Cowell. I remember saying to him "Look, radio is never going to play your music - The Teletubbies or Gary Wilmot", and he agreed with me and went down the TV route starting with Robson and Jerome and a terrible version of Unchained

Melody that nobody has ever played or liked since, but it went to No1 at the time, as have all his ghastly talent show winners.

And, of course, there is what I call the Vile Pervert element - anyone knowing that a project is anything to do with me won't touch it.

I remember, a few months after my release from prison in 2005, I was tipped off about a kid making interesting music on You Tube. I could have signed him and made him a huge star but he was only 12. I didn't go near him and when I told my probation lady she said "thank God". Had I done so, I would have been dragged back to jail. A couple of years later Usher and Scooter Braun picked him up. He was called Justin Bieber. He still is.

Alex Day did great, but decided the effort needed did not warrant the result and is now happily regarding music as a hobby and not a career.

When Surrey Police decided to have a second bite at my cherry they contacted everyone anywhere near me. One of the useless cops, Paul Slaughter, left a message for Alex to call him back which he did, brightly recording the entire conversation.

It is fascinating to hear - under the guise of wanting to find out whether I'd ever tried it on, Slaughter pushed away, despite Alex saying there had never been any such thing, as Tommy had also told Slaughter beforehand.

80
That's All Folks!

It is quite impressive actually.

At no point does Slaughter, clearly reading from a script, prod Alex into actually making an allegation. But it's clear that if Alex had said "I'd have to take time off work to come to the station", that Slaughter would have rapidly explained that Surrey Police would re-imburse any travel costs and that there might even be money in it ("compensation")…

but since Alex never went anywhere near there Slaughter, disappointed, never properly broaches the subject. Listening to the tape, the sub text is clear. And is just one of many reasons why the eventual charges were thrown out.

Police should not work from one side only. It is understandable that they do, and nobody could complain if genuine villains get trapped by cunning manoeuvring. It's gone on forever - even in the good old Dixon of Dock Green days.

But there has to be intelligent analysis behind it all - as you can see in the police report about liar X, regarding film releases. The guy was lying and would not shift his lies even when confronted by the truth. It's a common fault that all false accusers have - stick to their stories, no matter what they are faced with. In that case the officer, who I actually felt was a decent cop, concluded that, as a result, the man had been over 16 when he first met me and not 14, as he claimed.

A bent cop would probably have binned the evidence. And there are many of them - the majority, I suspect. Too lazy, too committed to the agenda, too concerned with getting off home to worry about convicting an innocent person. That attitude, understandably, poisons the entire system.

Slaughter was clearly not prepared to push Alex or Tommy into making false claims, no matter how tempting. Good for him. He was not a bent cop (though see elsewhere regarding his and his wife's tax payer paid trip to Italy). But a good cop, in several of these cases, should have said to their bosses "Look, it's obvious this man has never committed any of the crimes alleged - time to move on".

Did anyone ever do that? We shall never know. And it must be hard when your superiors are saying "Don't even consider he's innocent - your job is to find evidence that will get him convicted".

The Trans Gender issue is very strange. I don't understand it at all.

It may be an age thing.

Our human species exists and all humans have different levels of male and female in them. Both physically and emotionally.

In the good old days there were people described as

80
That's All Folks!

hermaphrodites. Either neither male nor female physically - or both. Perfectly possible. Just as there are people born without arms or with shorter limbs than others. Society should make sure everyone is treated with care and respect; dignity, assistance, adapting to the needs and abilities of others.

I've described elsewhere my friend Laurence - quadriplegic after an accident when he was 20. He coped brilliantly until Surrey Police came knocking when he was 56 - accusing him of the appalling crime of being a victim.

I was incredibly impressed how he had adapted, coped - and led an absolutely normal life.

I'm a big fan of JK Rowling's work - have been since the 1990s when I put out a compilation tribute to her Potter characters which was met at retail with "Who the fuck is Harry Potter?" I love her Strike novels. And agree with her - it's nonsense allowing people with penises to enter women's toilets or dressing rooms.

If someone like Charlie who, I assume, has a penis - I stress I have no first hand knowledge of this, wants to identify as a woman, fine by me. Although if I loved him/her and wanted him/her to become pregnant by me, it might be difficult. There is always adoption.

Sports. In my experience women trying to play mens sports rarely works. Oh it sometimes does - Martina was a great tennis player and incidentally a very nice person; I met her several times. But generally I don't enjoy them. Yes they can be better in some ways (tactics) but worse in others (stamina - women have muscles in different places to men).

As mentioned above, women are far better at bearing children. They are built for it. In many other ways, a female brain and body function differently to a male's - driving, for example.

Most women are dreadful drivers; most males are OK.

Oh yes. I'm well aware this is controversial. But I've examined drivers all over the world. I almost always drive, in whichever city or country I am in. I remember when they had just opened CHINA for visitors, it took no end of effort to hire a car but I managed it, actually driving out from Peking to the Great Wall of China, amongst other places.

I could not read the road signs and found it challenging, mainly because most other travellers were on bicycles - the things I most remember about that wonderful country are cabbages and bicycles. Whenever I got lost, I stopped and asked for directions. Without fail, people were helpful and friendly. Never once did I encounter unpleasantness. In fact several times I was invited into homes and given a meal. Or at least tea.

Likewise in India, where drivers were, then, an entire

80
That's All Folks!

category of employment - I ended up being given the Head of Sony, India, daughter's car. It was impossible to hire in fabulous Bombay, now called Mumbai, why do they all do this? I don't think Peking is Peking anymore. Why would anyone choose to remove a KING from their name?

I loved India; drove all over the place; the locals all found this highly amusing; my lovely hotel there, one of the best in the world, was later the subject of a terrorist attack.

But wherever I have gone, to this day, bad driving is frequently by a woman.

It must be part of the feminine mind set. I bet there were no female charioteers in Roman times.

Of course this is an exaggeration - there are some superb women drivers - my Mum was one. And, like everything else, it's degrees.

Producing records and directing movies - God knows why, but the male character seems generally better at that than women. Parenting - I'd say, generally, females make far better parents than males, especially for female kids. Politics and government - with exceptions, women are useless.

Maggie was brilliant, though I disagreed with her policies.

In fact let's pause here for a moment and think again

about Maggie. Margaret Thatcher. Very much a woman. But with a 10% masculine side. And as luck would have it, those masculine attributes included leadership.

We've had several other women PM's at time of writing. Theresa May. Dreadful with no leadership qualities whatsoever - she was also a woman but never had any children, adopted or otherwise, and seemed to have very few female attributes.

And Liz Truss. Bonkers. I don't think we need even call her a woman though my ex MP, Mark Field, might disagree. He went on to have problems with a woman later himself, rugby tackling a masked terrorist who could have been any of the several genders, which destroyed his career when it turned out it was a she, not a he. Which I would have thought was neither here nor there, a girlie being quite as able to murder someone as a boy, but what do I know? Media and society condemned Mark and made him the baddie. He lost his seat. It confused me.

Anyway I got to know Maggie quite well. After interviewing her for The Brits which I was salvaging - never had any thanks from the British public - we met up several times.

We disagreed on a lot of her policies and discussed, even argued, at length. I never got her to change her mind, not for a single second, and we did share very similar views on the economy. But above all she was a leader,

80
That's All Folks!

prepared to make decisions, right or wrong.

Also a very attractive lady. Not in the physically beautiful way but in the emotional, soulful way. And with a great sense of humour as described before. I was invited to several of those ghastly Downing Street parties - at every one she made me laugh.

Incidentally my dear friend Alan Rebbeck (Alice) worked as a waiter at some of those events. He told me numerous tales but the thing I most remember is how easy it was for someone to bypass security and infiltrate No10, as a temporary Member of Staff. It still, to this day, puzzles me how there hasn't been a terror strike on Downing Street and I bet it's the same in Washington.

Alan recently passed away, which allows me to reveal that.

But the point of this is to show - let's not be silly. A woman can have many masculine qualities, good and bad. And a man likewise - some of the best male leaders, even dictators, have great feminine qualities. Worrying about how you "self identify" is stupid.

So Charlie can be whatever he wants. Call himself whatever he wants. Dress and makeup however he wants. And ask me to treat him as male or female - it makes no difference. I shall treat him as a human being. That's what matters.

Funnily enough I have a similar situation with Alex,

who has decided he's a vegan. I can see no sense in veganism but if that's his choice, fine by me.

We've discussed it at length and agree to disagree. Moral-wise it is absurd - who says a carrot is less worthy of life than a chicken? Health-wise, ditto - no milk or honey? Bonkers. Unless you're lactic intolerant, in which case don't touch the stuff. I personally think it's more to do with wanting to be a member of a cult. A community. Be it Vegans or Trans or even, God forbid, online groups.

Each to their own. My only advice is - be true to yourself. And oddly that often means simply belonging, as an individual, to one cult. The human species.

As for Tommy, I have no idea what he's up to these days. After the call from Surrey Police, at which he told me he informed them I was the perfect gentleman, he's disappeared, changed his name and seems to have joined or formed a creative commune, making very obscure works of art in every direction.

I rather suspect the call terrified him so much that he decided to stay away from me as I was mad, bad and dangerous to know, all of which I totally agree with. Rather like my dear friend Simon Cowell, who was warned by his advisor Max Clifford, when he asked him about our friendship, to avoid perverts. And dear Samantha Fox who was told by Myra, her lover and manager in the early part of this century, that it might be

80
That's All Folks!

wiser not to be my friend.

I remember Tommy once raved about his new friend. "He's so lovely, JK; intelligent, sensitive, caring". "Have you met him?". "No, only online but he's so fantastic". Hmm.

I think both Tommy and Charlie personify their generations - now middle aged in their 30s and 40s, brought up, in their teens, based in a world of different values. You never need meet friends, as they do not, nor get involved in any depth, loyalty or real involvement.

Just like cartoon characters they can be lovely, intelligent, sensitive and caring - all superficial, unimportant qualities, easily abandoned, with as much worth as a plastic credit card. Which means, if they desert or betray you, who cares? You meant very little anyway.

That's why people are so mortified by online insults. I can never understand why? Their praise meant nothing. Why should their criticism? My friend (yes, in real life) Stephen Fry admits to being offended by online insults and hate. Why? Oh, the young!

It's not just the young. For decades, as media has grown more dominant, people tend to care what others think of them more than what we think of ourselves. Bound to end in tears.

Personally I don't mind what anyone calls me. Mistress King will do fine. I'll even accept Vile Pervert.

I'm a man but who cares? Sexually I'm bisexual and happy for everyone to know that except that, at 80, it's NO sexual coupled with CantBeBothered sexual.

But wisdom can come from experience, and it definitely has, for me. Years ago I became friendly with a young American called Steve Greenberg. Steve had made an album in 1993 using the lead singer of soul band The Chairmen of the Board - General Johnson - with the early punk outfit The Ramones. Called Rockaway Beach it was by The Godchildren Of Soul. Nobody liked it except me. I thought it was marvellous, promoted it in The Tip Sheet and helped it get released in the UK.

Steve went on to other labels and made a silly single with a group of kids called Hanson. It was called MmmBop. The Mercury label boss, Danny Goldberg, played it to me without much expectation and I went through the roof.

"That's brilliant! It's a smash!".
"Really? I just thought it was a silly novelty song".
"Novelty or not, it's a future No1".

Knowing I was often right, the label promoted it and it became huge. Steve went on to further success including Joss Stone, The Jonas Brothers and - for me - he then recorded The Baha Men with Who Let The Dogs Out? It took me eight dinners to convince him the song was a hit and eventually he told me that he simply didn't like

80
That's All Folks!

MY version but could he record the song with his group. "Sure - please do", I replied. It's sold 16 million copies so far.

But after Hanson's success, with the three young brothers including an 11 year old on drums, Steve said to me "I'll never produce kids again. The consequences can be appalling". He was right. I saw it with little Michael Jackson. The stresses and strains of fame, wealth and very adult work, with no time for play or, more important, learning, can be terminal.

I gather Hanson still exists as a group and the brothers are all OK. But I remember The Bay City Rollers, who I first produced, and the effects on members and linked executives. The Monkees, who I knew well. So many other child stars, often only booked because they looked cute and would appeal to teens and pre-teens, girls and boys. Today I watch TV shows made featuring middle aged or elderly women and men who once played a tiny part in a huge, marketed group and are now sad, wrinkled and old, disillusioned by failure.

Mind you, having said that, is it any worse than any other one-shot life?

And Charlie, mentioned above, would certainly have been destroyed by fame and celebrity. That was why I insisted Sons of Admirals broke up. They could have been One Direction. Look what happened there.

Yes; they made millions. Yes; many loved them. But after the inevitable break ups so many go off the rails. Drugs and alcohol play a big part. So do "friends" who are not real friends, even if they actually exist in the real world.

Liam Payne's death could have been predicted. Others will survive but decline. Celebrity is a terrible addiction for most people. I've mentioned before how police and people in authority start feeling ENABLED. They are entitled to a different level of respect, they think. Well, the same applies to success in careers or even in personal lives. We can all fall for it and many of us do.

Just a note after mentioning Rockaway Beach. I once met a fabulous 18 year old young man there. Gorgeous. I explained my scene and he wasn't interested in sex - he was still a virgin. But we liked each other and he agreed to join me for dinner.

We drove into Manhattan and to one of the top restaurants, owned by my friend from the 1960s, Keith McNally.

At another table, on his own, was Andy Warhol. I knew him through his fascination with The Bean. He would often phone us at home.

"What sort of a name is Whore Hole?".

"Stop it Jonathan; let me speak to The Bean".

After waving a greeting to Andy, the boy and I got on

80
That's All Folks!

with our meal. I explained to him what my life and career was. At one point he said "You must be famous. Andy Warhol can't stop looking over here at you".

I knew exactly why Andy kept looking over and it was nothing to do with me.

After a lovely dinner the boy said… "You know what JK? I've decided I'd like to try it once".

We went back to my apartment and had a wonderful session, after which I drove him back to Rockaway Beach.

"It was fantastic", he said, "but not really my scene. Thanks for letting me experience it though".

That sort of encounter has happened a lot in my life and I have very happy memories of every time.

JONATHAN KING

Chapter 19

PRIVATE INVESTIGATORS, POLICE AND CROOKED LAWYERS

When it all started, again, in 2015, as a direct result of the Jimmy Savile scandal, Jimmy having died, thus leaving libel-free legal excuse for enablers like Mark Williams Thomas to make a fortune, Surrey Police thought "we'll have some of that" and launched Operation Ravine, examining old, failed claims from the previous century.

As a result, little since 2015 appeared in my first two volumes of autobiography 65 and 70, though much was covered in GUILTY and in Not A Knee On The Neck, available from Amazon and most good bookstores.

When I was arrested in a blaze of publicity in 2015 - otherwise, what would have been the point? - an old friend from my music days got in touch with my brother Andy. Maggi Farran had been a first class plugger, press agent - or Promotion Person, in the 1970s. Also, whether or not it should be mentioned, very attractive. At one

80
That's All Folks!

point married to BBC producer Tony Wilson - not the TV presenter, who was another friend - Andy and he had been partners in an internet radio station joint venture, in the very early days, called Total Rock.

Maggi called Andy. She had left the music world years ago and was remarried to an ex New Zealand copper, now Private Investigator, called William Merritt. She was now Maggi Merritt.

When Dave Lee Travis had been arrested, Maggi had contacted him, as a mate from the BBC days, and suggested he take on the services of her husband to clear his name. Which he did, spectacularly.

For me perhaps the worst example of the broken British judicial system was how the CPS, failing on all counts with Travis, thrown out of court and declared Not Guilty of most claims, demanded and were given a retrial on two undecided counts, found an appalling comedienne, I use the word lightly, to adapt claims she had made in her comedy act into more serious allegations, and got a tiny conviction on that one pathetic count which resulted in no prison time at all but ruined his career and life and satisfied the CPS desire for convictions, at all costs, to boost their media image.

There have been many more spectacular miscarriages of justice for bigger names and those with no profile at all. And some acquittals, like my own. But I find the

Travis persecution, somehow, the most offensive of them all. Spiteful, nasty and showing all the worst aspects of the system. Those who want a conviction at all costs, whether true or false, running the world. What a terribly bad taste in the mouth for humanity.

I got on OK with Dave, whenever we met over the years, but he was not one of my friends. A bit of a lad; a burly bear of a man, not a great DJ but alright; quite tactile and clearly keen on the ladies. I tell, elsewhere, when he met my American girlfriend Janet, in his Top of the Pops dressing room, and charmed her whilst getting changed and flexing his muscles as he stripped off. "What a revolting man" said Janet, after we left.

But that is not what society should be all about. People with different attitudes but who are not offensive on any serious level must be accepted, not prosecuted. The current stupid habit of prosecuting people who disagree with you has become absurd and ridiculous. We Sixties kids could never have protested the Vietnam war. Before us, Germans could not have protested against Nazis as a few brave souls did. You can't believe we're on the eve of destruction takes on a whole new meaning in this self righteous century.

Absurd "scandals", like those destroying minor celebrities like the TV chef programme commentator Gregg Wallace and the delightful champion Wynne

80
That's All Folks!

Evans, completely take over and ruin careers and lives. Why? Because they are "great stories". I admire Trump, who I don't like at all and disagree with almost all his policies, because he took on both media and judges supporting the False Allegations Industry, and won, again and again.

Another DJ, who remains high profile, used to consider it hilarious when he exposed his penis to the radio newsreader during his show, trying to crack him or her up. Indeed that was a regular occurrence in the 60s and 70s. Sort of mooning - and there was a lot of that too. I never found it at all funny but I was never one of those types. These days nobody would dare do such things but that was then, this is now. It was a different morality then.

And just because it makes a good media story and titillates, us, the reader or viewer or listener, delighted by inflated celebrity damage, doesn't make it right.

It's still going on. Every day another face is "cancelled". Another singer or rapper is prosecuted. Protest is a crime. Aggressive lyrics are not only banned - they are crimes. For no good reason and often played wrongly by the wounded victims who inevitable apologise profusely - DON'T!! - and weep, saying they will never do it again. They won't - because we'll never hear from them again.

William then went on, after Travis, to work on the Rolf

Harris appeals - again, hugely successfully. I strongly recommend his book on Rolf. Essential reading on how an innocent man was convicted and ruined. If William had been on Rolf's side at the first trial, without a shadow of doubt Rolf would have been acquitted on all charges.

Merritt had been a police officer in New Zealand but, unlike most cops, I gather he was a very good one. Tall, decent looking, I think the words "senatorial" or "patrician" would suit him; never riled; calm and logical. Also very honest and honourable. When I took him on he said "JK I have to tell you that if I find evidence that proves to me you are guilty, I'll have to resign from the job. I can only ever work on something I have absolute total belief in. I hope you can appreciate that".

Private Investigators are a strange bunch. Most are totally useless. Trained as police officers, in itself a bad idea, and boasting of that, as a reason to trust them. Don't. They share, with the majority of cops, certain characteristics - laziness, do anything for money, the art of bluff and bluster, moral entitlement and greed - and, as I found in 2001, are also usually very bad at their jobs.

I've told before that, in that trial, one of my false accusers who, admittedly, had a common name, was found to have been fundamentally dishonest and had a conviction for robbery - important, as my accuser worked in a well known high street bank. We sprang that on him

80
That's All Folks!

in cross examination. Unfortunately it backfired. It wasn't him. Same name but totally different location.

The Court fell silent. I could see jurors shift sides. We had egg on our faces, totally due to the inept work of the (expensive) Private Investigator, taken on by my (expensive) solicitor on the advice of my (expensive) QC - I've since discovered most lawyers have pet PI's, most useless (and expensive) to whom they owe favours.

My fault. Had I known then what I know now, it would have taken me seconds of internet investigation, even back then when it was all Yahoo and AOL with no You Tube or Google, to have discovered that the information was WRONG!

Cut to 2015 and, thanks to the Magnificent Maggi, I could take on William. I went out to their beautiful home, played with their beautiful Belgian Shepherd dog Harry, explained the specifics I needed to William and off he went.

After my total acquittal in 2018, when HHJ Taylor, impressed by the evidence amassed by our defence on all the False Accusers, or "victims", refused the CPS application for any retrials under any circumstances, I called Wills to thank him for his incredible work.

"Not at all, JK", he replied, "it wasn't down to me at all. I just did my job".

"Do you credit the lawyers?" I asked. My team -

Steven Bird, Henry Blaxland and Alexandra Felix, had been pretty good but not fantastic.

"No", said Wills, who greatly admired the QC Stephen Vullo on other cases including the second Rolf Harris trial in 2017, and had liked my team - "you. JK. You told me exactly what you needed in detail, we went and did exactly as you requested". Apart from anything else, how refreshing to hear someone refuse to take credit for something.

In his experience, and mine, most lawyers simply give the PI a vague brief ("find something on Jones") and send them off. One reason he liked Vullo was that he didn't do that - like me, he gave specifics. I'm sure that legal vagueness was what happened in 2001, with the bank clerk. Lawyers have too many cases, too little time and really cannot be bothered. Also, let's be honest, they just don't know the truth, as opposed to the lies.

Example - one False Accuser in 2018 used his then, first, girlfriend, to whom he and she had both lost their virginity, as a crucial example in his sworn police statement, since he had used a condom I had bought for him at his request. Police searched for her for weeks. Having married and changed her name, this proved impossible, they said.

It took William and his team five minutes. He found her, visited her; got a sworn, signed statement, which

80
That's All Folks!

proved incredibly useful, and delivered it to me and eventually to my defence team, to the court and to God Almighty. Yes; but years later than claimed. Yes; I had provided the condom under the strict condition that both he and his partner had to have been over 16 - they were a week under that age and had laughed about it.

So why couldn't police do that? First, because I suspect they were well aware she might destroy the prosecution case (NOTE: surely police should be balanced - investigating both sides of an allegation). Second, because PLOD are generally useless ("find someone who has changed her name? Impossible").Third, because they don't care. Just another job. Have a coffee.

Another vital witness in the same fake claim involved a school friend of the false accuser. That was harder. No trace of somebody clearly keen to leave no footprint online. William's team came up with nobody for a long time, despite working like mad. We gave up.

Then, just the other day, beavering away as I'm quite good at this online thing, thanks to Mr Murdoch getting me, as a SUN columnist, to go online with my column filed on a Tandy each week, I tracked him down on his new Facebook page. That's part of the problem - so many sites now - Instagram, X you name it.

But still no contact information. Then…

A photo he had taken and put up recently of his hotel

room. There, lying on the desk, his driving licence and registration card. With all contact details. Zoom in.

William is onto it.

The point is - and DO read his Rolf Harris book; it explains so much - a good Private Investigator is worth his weight in gold. I have no idea how Kevin Spacey's cases are going - having been acquitted several times, the bent and corrupt enablers are still after him.

Unless everything has been settled out of court, as it usually is, in civil cases, see elsewhere - and should NEVER be; never pay off a blackmailer, he really ought to talk to William Merritt. And when he does, go through in detail the truth and the areas of provable lies.

It is really quite easy to show that liars are fundamentally dishonest and, broken though the judicial system may be, Judges and Juries do not like fundamentally dishonest people. Which most accusers often are.

I'm sure this is a global problem. And I'm sure even hugely wealthy defendants like Jeffrey Epstein or Harvey Weinstein, are unaware of just how vital, and how rare, a good private investigator is. Hit by these appalling claims, backed by experienced and devoted enablers, supported by police, backed by virtually every media, social and traditional - we victims of false accusers tend to go numb.

We have never experienced anything like it. Neither

80
That's All Folks!

have "normal" people - for them it is even more terrifying. Those with money rely on others to deal with it and those are usually useless "yes men and women".

Those without rely on Legal Aid or the equivalent and so few of those are even competent, let alone willing to do a job for little financial reward. So the miscarriages of justice pile up. Not just sex cases. Murders. Fraud. Cyber crime.

I think it is a CRIME. Colluded by defence lawyers who make a fortune. By the Courts, who believe they must obey the protocol even if it is the modern equivalent of blackmail - as I've said, using the law to break the law.

Judges will say that everybody must be entitled to justice but, in civil cases, this rarely happens and the blackmailers, or their enablers, are rarely prosecuted. No Win No Fee should not be a way of letting a criminal commit a crime. It has frequently become just that.

This is a massive problem which is insidiously destroying humanity. Good people are brought down by failing to defend themselves properly. Again, read Bob Woffinden's book The Nicholas Cases. Your jaw will drop.

Why on earth would anybody with a brain cell be a teacher these days? Or a doctor or a foster parent? Or a vicar or priest? Or even (who cares?) a TV personality or DJ or pop star?

It really should not be necessary. Innocent until and unless proven guilty. Allegations should be investigated in a balanced way and either rejected or pursued, if there is evidence. False accusers should be prosecuted, as with every other crime. Media will say "but then the guilty will get away with it" - 'twas always so. We need strong, good, honest police investigators who will at least try to unearth the truth.

So why is it happening? Two reasons - first, times change. Morals change. Acceptable past behaviour, like trying to attract someone you find attractive, is no longer allowed. But that's only fine if prosecution and complaints only apply to now, to the current social norms.

Secondly - the media (and most of us) prefer highly inflated and exaggerated stories. So it is simply not enough to say somebody "tried it on" 40 years ago. Their attempt, if one was made, must be for rape, and violent rape at that. "A wank would have sufficed" is not, as your KC will inform you, a wise defence.

In a courtroom such a thing will become clear, it will be said by those protecting the status quo. But watching video of some stupid male drag his stupid wife or stupid girlfriend back to their hotel room is only evidence of extremely rude and bad mannered behaviour. Extremely wealthy man treating extremely greedy woman very

80
That's All Folks!

badly. If a complaint is made within hours, it could well then be evidence of possible, subsequent worse actions. Days later - it's still pretty lethal. Months or years later - it should not be worth so much.

Guilty of appalling, toxic activity, probably. Evidence of anything else? No. Did this prove he then raped her in the privacy of his room? No. But most people, persuaded by a decent prosecutor, think it does.

Just try to explain that to a jury. After weeks of extreme media coverage and much affecting court room action, preferably featuring sobbing, tears, running mascara and break downs, any sensible person will believe anything. Especially if women or children are involved. Sweet, fragile, innocent, honest victims? Not always.

But that is, surely, not as it should be. Root and branch change are vital to the system. I stress - I know nothing. But I've seen it at first hand I know what goes on. So has Andrew Malkinson, whose interview in The Times is essential reading for anyone who cares. As he does. Not just for him. Not just for me. But for all the current and past victims and the millions of future ones to come, if this is allowed to continue.

Chapter 20

I AM ABOUT TO DIE

This is not a suicide note. I certainly have no intention to leave you just yet. But it happens. An old friend just died, aged 88.

My mother died at 91 but told me "You don't want to live beyond 80" and I know what she meant. You run out of energy. Breathing gets difficult. You have to sit down a lot. Most of my age group uses a crutch or two or even a Zimmer frame.

Being massaged recently, at the Villa Cora in Florence, I reminded the young masseuse that, a couple of years ago, she had told me "you have the body of a 40 year old".

"It's true", she answered. "At least the **suppleness** of a 40 year old. I can twist you and bend you as though you are under 40. Oh yes, your skin is that of a 60 year old, but you are incredibly supple".

Funnily enough the dead friend, mentioned above,

80
That's All Folks!

first turned me onto the wonderful Cavalieri Hilton Hotel in Rome back in 1966. I was heading to Italy for a holiday. Andrew told me "You must stay at the Cavalieri Hilton - best view in Rome". And I did - actually with best hotel room view in the **world** overlooking all seven hills or at least six - it's on Monte Mario which may be one of the seven. Indeed, rumour has it that the wolves who brought up Romulus and Remus - they didn't - it's a fable, like Jesus - lived on this very hill.

With a fabulous pool. I'm there every day every summer, at this very moment as my digits click the laptop keys. I used to swim 5 hours a day - breast stroke, calm and slow like a dowager duchess. I'm still like a duchess, but only manage about 2 hours a day.

My times in sunshine used to be just July in summer and leaving on Boxing Day after spending Christmas with my Mum and, later, numerous nephews, god children and others, whose joy at that young age seemed to be unwrapping presents and not the gifts inside. A month in Morocco.

It expanded. These days, if possible, it's four months in summer - May, June, July, August and two in winter December and January. Six months swimming in blazing sunshine. Keeps me healthy.

Andrew was one of many queens older than me, and thus still of the generation for which being gay was a sin and a crime. As a result they knew all about the best places around the globe for fairies to visit or live - just read Joe Orton's diaries - like Tangier, for so many expatriates, and the countries with more advanced rules and laws about same sex adventures. It was Andrew who introduced me to Nino Mulas - see earlier volumes.

The Cavalieri remains magnificent. I can no longer afford to stay there, but they do a special Members Spa deal for a month at a time, so I still use the facilities daily.

I'm convinced swimming for half each year has kept me alive. Along with never smoking or doing drugs. Or being angry. Bile kills. I even managed to swim in prison in one of the few jails with a pool - HMP Maidstone. I wonder if it's still there. Very few inmates ever used it - only me and a couple of officers, or screws as they are fondly known.

I've never used recreational drugs. Oh I take dozens of medical tablets every day - statins, glucose control, vitamins - but as I reached both the worlds of university - jazz was big in the early 1960s, as was the use of drugs in jazz and around jazz - and music - LSD arrived; everyone smoked pot; Mama Cass desperately tried to turn me on in the Hamburger Hamlet - see elsewhere - I clearly needed to make up my mind.

Was I going to get into it, like all my friends? Or not? I decided NOT. Mainly because I felt life had so much

80
That's All Folks!

to offer, I didn't want to conceal or confuse it with a smoke screen of brain altering chemicals. My Mother and Father both smoked, which had put me off. So had my experience under the bridge as a 5 or 6 year old when I won a bet - "you can't get through a whole packet in 5 minutes" - I did, by eating them and was violently ill for days. Also I knew these strange elements had not been fully tested or examined. Alcohol was poison. Nicotine gave you cancer. Marijuana affected the brain. Why allow any of them to enter my body?

I never preached to anyone else, and have never concealed my decision. And I have to say - so many friends and even total strangers either died or became incredibly confused. Mick Jagger was always a great example of using drugs and not letting them use him - I attended many meetings with him, he never was stoned. But his complexion became ruined, lined with a million creases like an ancient monkey. Just read a long interview with Heston Blumenthal - who seems to have almost killed himself with cocaine. All that snorting - why? Like heroin - needles! Why?

Different strokes for different folks.

Almost every one of my false accusers had experiences with drugs or alcohol long before they met me, if they ever did meet me. Indeed, some have long medical histories of drugs or drink problems - losing jobs;

wrecking marriages; criminal convictions - every one admitting they started addictions long before bumping into me, if they ever did bump into me.

And linking up with a religion or cult or philosophy usually brings simple solutions to complex problems. One vegan friend of mine (Alex Day who, editing this, has allowed me to "credit" him), when I asked "why can't you drink milk?", replied "because it's meant for calves".

Had no answer as to "meant by whom?". Or "does everything have to have only one purpose?". My poor penis, only meant to piss, has been sorely misused for several other functions. Never meant - by whoever.

The answer is - "there's no point in discussing it. You won't change your mind". I would if someone could simply say "I believe there's a God or Creator or Guru or whatever and they made this world and they said milk can only be drunk by calves". OK if that's your belief, live by it, fair enough. But don't use logic like that to try to convince me - or, worse, yourself.

"Milk is not healthy", they will say. It is for me. Though clearly not for a lactic intolerant. Like peanut allergy, horses for courses. But general rules, be they food and drink or laws and crimes, ought never to exist without individual qualifications.

Someone at 15 might be both physically and emotionally able to have sex. Someone at 22 may not - on

80
That's All Folks!

both counts. And can you imagine having to live without honey? A land of milk and honey = paradise.

I remember Scott Walker, my dear friend in the 1960s, once tried to get me drunk. We were on holiday in Sitges, Spain, sharing a hotel room and, indeed, the same bed, though nothing sexual had happened.

Looking back, we both wanted it but neither dared go for it. I'd deliberately made contact with him because he was gorgeous as lead singer of The Walker Brothers. He'd reciprocated because so was I - then a smash hit singer and writer at No1 on the charts. We then became dear friends, like brothers. I've discussed Scott elsewhere but looking back, his attempt to get me smashed on tequila worked, but made me totally unconscious, hung over and determined never to touch the stuff again. No sex. It would have been impossible. My dick was then pickled and permanently flaccid.

Same holiday, by the sea in a hire car, he said he had to take a shit. We were at one end of the beach; the car blocked him from view from most bathers but he insisted I stood guard on his side, watching for anybody nearby. I told him this was disgusting as he dropped the longest, largest turd I've ever seen and covered it with sand. Despite this romantic interlude, our bromance never became a romance, I suspect to both our disappointment.

Sorry if I've alluded to this elsewhere. I keep forgetting

things and was recently convinced I have Alzheimers - early onset. As I've described before - my doctor sent me to the top consultant in the UK. Whilst I have no sign of senility, my age does mean I cannot keep recent events or comments in my head and he was prepared to write a report for me on that, in case I ever have to suffer fresh criminal or civil cases.

Very kind of him though I'm not sure, if any claim DOES end up in court instead of being "settled on the court room steps" as the crooked lawyers expect, that any judge would allow such specialist, expert evidence.

Because it would set a precedent. And thousands of past cases would be overturned. Not, in judicial or government eyes, a good thing. But, as Sir Brian Leveson points out in his excellent review of the Court process, adapting is vital and essential.

Our old rules and laws simply no longer hold water in this century. Just as the Internet has produced, as a side effect, a source for fundamentally dishonest people and their enablers to produce evidence of a crime - how on earth can she have known he was doing a personal appearance in Portsmouth unless she was there, being assaulted?

One click finds the facts and often even photos. As can cameras - everywhere now. All too easy to make a logical step from "Yes he WAS in Portsmouth" to "Therefore he

80
That's All Folks!

must have raped her". And when he says "I can't remember being in Portsmouth" for a prosecutor to say or imply he was trying to evade the truth.

I suppose it's like an old car. Bits start falling off. Tubes get clogged up. Joints and muscles ache. And there are all the nasty diseases that come along as the years go by - almost Marianne Faithful 1965.

I want to keep going. There is so much needing to be achieved. Slowly but surely, like in Malkinson. Like the Lucy Letby case, currently causing a lot of previously convinced media people and even past ministers to become seriously unconvinced. Like the Post Office scandal.

But I hasten to add - virtually everything I've done this century has flopped.

Books, TV, videos, music, nothing has caught fire commercially. That's not to say creatively; I'm proud of what I've done since I was 56 when Max Clifford and Surrey Police changed the direction of my career in music. A young friend recently told me I'd be very, very famous and acclaimed - after my death. And I think he may be right. Not that I haven't achieved quite a lot in my first 80 years - he wasn't around in the 60s, 70s or 80s of course.

Let's be honest, 90s stuff like Eurovision, The Brits and other moments mean little to today's young. Many of them have never even heard Who Let The Dogs Out? Or I Get Knocked Down But I Get Up Again. Let alone Everyone's Gone To The Moon or It's Good News Week. "Someone's dropped a bomb somewhere contaminating atmosphere"? These days - a **CRIME** even to comment on such a thing. Unless it's in Gaza of course.

So - should I blame the events of 2000 and 2001? For 25 years of abject failure?

No. I've been busy. I still have a great time. I observe. I comment. I opine. If only a few give a damn, fine by me. It's the doing that gives pleasure and satisfaction - Bubblerock 1971. Profits can be more than money.

And I sometimes look at people who are my age and have done the same thing, or variations of it, for all of their lives. And are now nearing the end. Do they feel they've wasted the gift of life? Or has it been hugely rewarding for them too? Let's be frank - I've not done a lot of things myself. Never fathered children. Never had grand children. Who Do I Think I Are? It stops here, girls, goes no further. Future makers of that show won't have anybody tracing their ancestry to me and beyond. End of the line.

That's All, Folks.

I don't want to be boring - how could that ever be? But what is the point of life? Well, I reckon it's to enjoy the variety of experiences and sensations of being a

80
That's All Folks!

human. So much to appreciate, of every kind.

Next; it's to have personal relationships. Mine have been fantastic and thanks to all those who have contributed to it on every level. Every single level. This final volume of autobiography is dedicated to every one of you. But especially to The Bean.

Then it's career. The chosen area of life - mine was and still is - COMMUNICATION. You're reading this. I'm communicating with you. And for me it's also a variety of communications. Singing and writing hits - my voice sold 40 million records after all. Under a variety of names. I watch concerts and festivals and see singers who have sold far, far fewer records and been on far, far fewer radio and TV smash hits than me.

If I headlined Glastonbury, my set would go on into the next day if I only sang the Top 50 hits I've recorded or been involved in. Fortunately that will never happen. Me on Glastonbury? Hold the front page. As well as singing and writing flops - my best record, I think, was A Very Very Melancholy Man - never a hit. And hardly even sung. Spoken or, rather, rapped.

Producing - my favourite role. And in doing so launching the careers of others - Genesis, 10cc, Abba etc… As dear Richard O'Brien said to me a few months ago "You contributed far more to the success of The Rocky Horror Show than almost everyone else JK". Let's

JONATHAN KING

do the Time Warp again.

Making films and writing books and columns and articles - another form of communication. Taking on Eurovision and winning for the UK. Salvaging The Brits. Having the top rated TV series Entertainment USA and many others - No Limits; The Record of the Year. A weekly page for ten years in The Sun, when it sold millions of copies ("best fucking thing in the paper" Rupert Murdoch). I read obituaries of people who had a couple of hits - puffed out for pages, avoiding the fact that they only sang or played on two million sellers. That, in itself, hardly enough to warrant a line of comment after death.

Having sex and giving pleasure - the ultimate communication. Friendship - a hugely important aspect of communication. I've had, and still have, some amazing friendships.

I'm not saying my chosen career was better or worse than yours. If you chose to be a street sweeper, have loved every second of your work, wouldn't have changed it for the world, it was just a different career - no better, no worse. It's the satisfaction that counts.

And if your relationships were fulfilling and brought joy to all concerned; if LOVE was encountered, experienced and enjoyed. If, on your death bed, it's coming to all of us, you feel you'll be able to say "I lived life to the full - to MY full", that was it.

80
That's All Folks!

BUT - were you a one hit wonder? Or even, a NO-Hit wonder. Was your life actually unfulfilling, boring, full of never achieved desires?

I remember Tony Blackburn on dear old Radio London used to chide me for being a One Hit Wonder after Everyone's Gone To The Moon, as indeed I was, as a singer - I'd had my second No1 as writer and producer weeks later with It's Good News Week. Tony always wanted to be a pop star and never was. A very successful DJ though, still on Radio Two as I write.

It took me a few more years to chart under my own name with the single Let It All Hang Out in 1970. "I preach, my dear friends…"

Did you always want to visit Hawaii but never did? Or eat a Michelin three star meal and never did? Or have sex with somebody gorgeous and never did? Have you read a book and gasped at how good it was? Watched a movie or TV show and been amazed by the artistic triumph? I did that with Adolescence last year. Or produced a family, been deeply in love, been the best parent, or child, ever - and never did? If you've simply existed, then that is a wasted life.

I loved Michael Jackson saying "Are you Jonathan King? I've always wanted to meet you" when he was a little boy or Marlene Dietrich saying "You are a poet and a genius" or Clem Cattini, one of the all time best drummers, telling me all the UK session musicians thought I was the best producer they ever worked with - later confirmed by the brilliant bass player Herbie Flowers on the phone to me, just before he died.

But, equally, those poor souls in prison. whose lives were so improved by my helping them read and write letters to loved ones and those loved ones, sometimes including young teenage sons, rushing up to me in the Visitors Room and hugging me and thanking me. How rewarding is that? And the thousands of future men and women released from jail because of my setting a precedent and getting changes made? How satisfying will that be?

And human beings, reading this tome in the future, long after I'm dead, and saving our species, and every other species, because of what they have learned from these words. Decency, kindness, tolerance. Even to the very worst?

So what happened to me, in my wasted life? And why?

Well, it appears that, after a pretty successful and varied existence, mainly in communication and personally, socially, I was due to move into a higher executive area of music - saving a giant record company, that had been the home of The Beatles amongst others. Probably merging EMI into the old Decca label too, which would have been purchased for next to nothing

80
That's All Folks!

from Universal, who had and have no idea what to do with it.

Rejuvenating the industry by forming downloads/uploads/streaming and saving retail at the same time, transforming it from basic sales to a series of go-to internet facilities run by music lovers. And benefitting the United Kingdom by billions of quids, plus creating millions of happy, fulfilling jobs.

It came crashing down but I've never resented it - though I was and remain innocent of the convictions against me, I deliberately broke the stupid law that condemned males over 21 and not females at 16. It gave me a new direction which I've pursued aggressively and hope to continue doing so.

Though it will need your help. I'm happy to lay the foundations but you need to build a decent, caring society.

Now that will really be satisfying. Over to you.

INDEX

A
ABBA – p.33, 37, 52, 78, 116, 119, 300
American Field Service – p.4
Are You Sure? – Eurovision – p.30
Attila the Hun – p.15

B
Band Aid / Live Aid – p.48
Bay City Rollers – p.52
Beastie Boys – p.20
Beatles – p. 29, 103, 105, 110, 126, 128, 207, 303
Bee Gees – p.24
Belfast – Eurovision – p.33
Bowie, David – p.40–53
　early career – p.42–46
　Glass Spider tour – p.48–49
　personal reflections – p.43–44
　sexuality and ambition – p.45–48

C
CCRC – p.57, 64–70, 88, 90, 98, 192
Chumbawumba – p.77, 204
Clifford, Max – p.56–57, 97, 121, 166, 203, 210, 259, 273, 298
Cottaging – p.23, 25–27
Crime and false accusations – p.54–57
Croix de Guerre – p.4

D
Davis, Clive – p.19, 27
Day, Doris – p.116, 123
Dean, Mr (schoolmaster) – p.6

80
That's All Folks!

Denning, Chris – p.57, 125, 130
Dickens, Charles – p.43
Dietrich, Marlene – p.116, 302

E–G
Education – childhood and school experiences – p.3–9
EMF – Unbelievable – p.21, 24
EMI Records – job offer – p.55
Entertainment USA – p.49, 79, 185, 301
Epstein, Brian – p.29, 41, 103-108, 128, 181, 194
Frampton, Peter – p.50
Fox, Sam – p.92–93, 150, 237, 263, 273
Friendship – value of – p.53
Fury, Billy – p.129
Gambaccini, Paul – p.86
Garfunkel, Art – Bright Eyes – p.18
Geldof, Bob – Live Aid – p.49, 213
Gina G – p.31, 80
Gloria – p.30

H–M
Hendrix, Jimi – p.107
Homosexuality and law – p.13
Houston, Whitney – p.19
Jackson, Michael – p.18, 37, 276, 302
Jagger, Mick – p.48, 294
John, Elton – p.49, 73, 113, 197, 208
King's Army – music promotion – p.58, 75, 179, 214
Liddiment, David – Eurovision – p.30
Live Aid – criticisms – p.48
Media criticism – p.15, 36, 38

INDEX

Michael, George – p.15–27
Morgan, Piers – p.187
Murdoch, Rupert – p.185-186, 227, 286, 301
Music Echo – column – p.41
Music industry – behind the scenes – p.35

N–S
Napier-Bell, Simon – p.20
Oasis – critique of popularity – p.36
Parmes, Larry – p.29
Phonogram – 10cc contract – p.17
Pirate Radio – p.125–126
Positive Discrimination – critique of – p.22–23
Presley, Elvis – p.3, 126
Prince Of Wales – p.43
Prison – legal battle references – p.64–70
Public toilets – cottaging – p.25–27
Rocky Horror Show – p.52, 116, 119, 198, 227, 300
Ronson, Mick – Bowie bandmate – p.47
Savile, Jimmy – p.15–17, 23, 46, 127, 165, 166, 181, 244, 251, 279
Sealey, Christopher – false accusation – p.66
Sexual experiences – early life reflections – p.14–15
Sexuality – societal and legal shifts – p.13–15, 83–84
Simone, Nina – p.116
Sinatra, Frank – p.116
Springfield, Dusty – p.21, 129–130, 207
Springsteen, Bruce – p.37, 71, 122
Street-Porter, Janet – p.33
Swift, Taylor – p.35, 114, 204, 264

80

That's All Folks!

T–Z

Thatcher, Margaret – p.71 –72, 271
Thailand – comments on sexuality and culture – p.45
Tootal – shirt company – p.4, 106
Transgender – p.264, 267
Trump, Donald – p.18
Turner, Simon – p.48
Una Paloma Blanca – p.30, 76
VICTIM (film) – p.25–26
Walker, Scott – p.130, 296
WHAM – early career and CBS support – p.19
Who Let the Dogs Out – p.52, 114, 204, 275, 299
Woffinden, Bob – p.64, 96, 188, 217, 255, 288
Woke culture – critique of – p.22
Yentob, Alan – Eurovision opposition – p.32, 77, 79